# HARLEM

# STOMP!

A CULTURAL HISTORY OF THE HARLEM RENAISSANCE

# HARLEM STOMP!

by LABAN CARRICK HILL

Megan Tingley Books
LITTLE, BROWN AND COMPANY
Books for Young Readers
New York   Boston

Little, Brown and Company
Hachette Book Group
1290 Avenue of the Americas, New York, NY 10104
Visit us at LBYR.com

Little, Brown and Company is a division of Hachette Book Group, Inc.
The Little, Brown name and logo are trademarks of Hachette Book Group, Inc.

The publisher is not responsible for websites (or their content) that are not owned by the publisher.

Originally published in hardcover by Little, Brown and Company in January 2004
This Paperback Edition: November 2020

The Library of Congress has cataloged the hardcover edition as follows:
Hill, Laban Carrick.
Harlem stomp! : a cultural history of the Harlem Renaissance/
by Laban Carrick Hill. — 1st ed.
p. cm.
Includes bibliographical references and index.
ISBN 978-0-316-81411-9 (hc)
ISBN 978-0-316-03424-1 (pb)
1. African Americans — Intellectual life — 20th century —
Juvenile literature. 2. Harlem Renaissance — Juvenile literature. 3.
African American arts — History — 20th century — Juvenile literature.
4. Harlem (New York, N.Y.) — Intellectual life — 20th century
— Juvenile literature. 5. African Americans — New York (State)
— New York — Intellectual life — 20th century — Juvenile literature.
6. African American arts — New York (State) — New York —
History — 20th century — Juvenile literature. 7. New York (N.Y.)
— Intellectual life — 20th century — Juvenile literature. I. Title.
E185.6 .H515 2004
810.9'896073 — dc21                          2002073067

ISBN: 978-0-316-49633-9


10 9 8 7 6 5 4

1010

Printed in China
The text was set in Granjon and Agenda,
and the display types are Parisian and Lithos.

Art direction by Alyssa Morris
Design by Elise Whittemore-Hill

## ACKNOWLEDGMENTS

Without Elise Whittemore-Hill and her support, insight, and incredible design, this book would not be what it is today. I would also like to thank Susan Cohen for her criticism and amazing faith, Megan Tingley for her superb editing, Jennifer Hunt for her outstanding editing and guidance to make this book happen, Alyssa Morris for her great art direction, Alvina Ling for her excellent editorial work, and Christine Cuccio for her eagle eye and unerring copy-editing. Dr. Lorrie Smith, St. Michaels College, provided support and criticism from the first idea for this book through to the last draft of the manuscript. Dr. Emily Bernard, University of Vermont, provided a wizened pair of eyes by reading the final manuscript and ensuring its accuracy. Finally, I'd like to thank the people who make writing worthwhile: Susan Thames, Joy Tomchin, and my daughters Natalie and Ella.

# CONTENTS

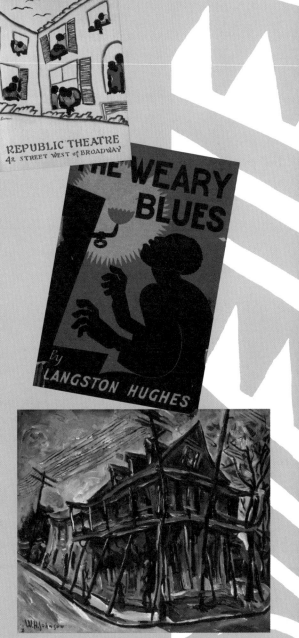

Harlem Plains before development, 1812.

Nail and Parker's "Big Deal," W. 113th St., 1915.

# FOREWORD

One of the most exciting periods in American History, if not in the history of the world, is the Harlem Renaissance. In the early part of the twentieth century, Harlem was a hotbed of intellectual, artistic, literary, and political blossoming for Black people. In response to the Black codes that were designed to undo the progressive 13th, 14th, and 15th Amendments to the Constitution, the Black population started voting with its feet and walking away from the brutality and hardships of the South. One can almost hear them ask, "Shall we gather at the river?" before they marched to the North. No matter what price they might have to pay, gather they did. They came to St. Louis, Chicago, and ultimately to Harlem seeking peace, prosperity and freedom. Stepping out on faith, they both preserved and created a culture. A people who were chattel only a generation earlier took over the cultural quilt of America and warmed the world.

It is an amazing piece of propaganda that Black people were lazy. Aside from the obvious impossibility that a slave cannot be alive and lazy, the fact is Blacks have worked, and worked hard and successfully, in every field of endeavor they have been allowed to pursue. What a crazy irony that the people who had faithfully cleared the forest and planted the very crops that would be staples of the young country, who had valiantly fought in each war, who had remained good and faithful friends through natural and manmade disasters, were now subject to unspeakable crimes. Blacks—who were lynched, bombed, and burned out by Whites for trying to exercise basic citizenship rights, and then had to watch those same terrorists claim that Blacks were not able and did not want to vote, go to school, or participate in the life of the community and country—were aghast at the blasphemy. Blacks had had enough. They left for the cities. They left for their physical and emotional well-being. They left to give their children a better chance.

There can be no doubt that they were scared. They had nothing but their great hearts,

which had carried them through two hundred of the darkest years of Euro-American history. How these years came to be years of shame for Black people is beyond understanding. It is not we who kidnapped, raped, and ravished a people. It is not we who continue to struggle against equality and opportunity.

The Harlem Renaissance is a testament to Black people's perseverance. It's a sounding call of Black innovation, freedom, and creativity. In music, the Harlem Renaissance brought together a gaggle of Blacks who sang their plantation songs and then made a variation called *blues* and then made a variation called *jazz*. The *Spirituals* and *jazz* are now considered American music, but that can only be true if Blacks are an American people.

The Renaissance can also be viewed through its literature. It was a great literature that was nurtured and created. Countee Cullen poignantly remembered a visit to Baltimore; Claude McKay in his famous poem "If We Must Die" demanded, "if we must die let it not be like hogs"; Zora Neale Hurston brought her keen observations to life and laughed at everybody; and the incomparable Langston Hughes wanted ultimately to know "What Happens to a Dream Deferred?" In his beautiful and eloquent poem "The Negro Speaks of Rivers," Hughes, like his peers, found the voice of justice, the voice of hope, and put it into words that others would hear, identify with, and understand. Visual artists, such as Aaron Douglas, had to overcome the negative images that had been perpetuated during slavery and Reconstruction. Movies like *Birth of a Nation* and *Gone with the Wind* had to be countered with true images of a people struggling to find a place for themselves in a nation ashamed of its past. *Harlem Stomp!* celebrates these brave and wonderful people. *Harlem Stomp!* finds both truth and joy in the struggle of rebirth. *Harlem Stomp!* is an American history of an American people redefining this great American nation.

—Nikki Giovanni

Aaron Douglas illustration from December 1925 *Opportunity* cover.

# SONG OF SMOKE

## THE SMOLDERING BLACK CONSCIOUSNESS, 1900–1910

I am the Smoke King

I am black!

. . . . . . . . . .

I will be black as blackness can —

The blacker the mantle, the mightier the man!

My purpl'ing midnights no day dawn may ban.

— W. E. B. DU BOIS, from "The Song of Smoke"

## FUELING THE EMBERS OF BLACK PRIDE

IN THE 1920s, Harlem was hot! The streets were crowded. The nightclubs were hoppin'. The theaters were packed to the rafters. And the poems and stories crackled with racial pride. Without a doubt Harlem was the center of the universe if you were black or just a white hepcat from downtown who knew where the action was. Nineteen twenties Harlem represented the coming of age for African Americans. And that time would come to be known as the Harlem Renaissance.

# "The problem of the Twentieth Century is the problem of the color-line —

The renaissance, however, didn't just blare out of Louis Armstrong's horn or spill from Langston Hughes's pen. The Harlem Renaissance was the culmination of a change in attitude that had begun two decades earlier. It was a shift in philosophy from accommodating white domination to demanding equal status and recognition for blacks. Critic W. E. B. Du Bois (doo-BOYZ) became one of the major voices of this new attitude when he first stated plainly the conflict that was to define much of the twentieth century in his groundbreaking book *The Souls of Black Folk*: "The problem of the Twentieth Century is the problem of the color-line — the relation of the darker races to the lighter races of men. . . ." When Du Bois wrote these words in 1902, they were not simply controversial. They were as radical as any statement a black man ever made publicly, because Du Bois was saying clearly that blacks could not be ignored any longer.

Booker T. Washington was a member of the older generation, born into slavery, who believed racial agitation was a course for disaster.

Since the emancipation of slaves in 1863, the traditional doctrine of race relations was one of accommodation. For blacks that meant: Don't make any waves and you won't be lynched. ("Lynch" means to put someone to death by mob action without legal authority.) Booker T. Washington, the most prominent African American at the time, strongly supported the principle of nonconfrontation. In his famous speech at the Atlanta Exposition on September 18, 1895, he said:

**"The wisest among my race understands that the agitation of questions of social equality is the extremest folly."**

Washington was a practical man. When he looked at African Americans, he saw a people barely able to survive. To his logic, what African Americans needed most were jobs, not equality. They needed to put food on the table and pay the rent. Consequently, he founded Tuskegee Normal School (now Tuskegee University), which trained blacks for jobs as teachers and later as maids, carpenters, and other manual laborers. Washington believed that to pursue any higher learning was not only impractical but dangerous for blacks.

A member of the first generation of blacks to have been born free, as well as the first African American ever to receive a Ph.D., Du Bois was deeply

Chicago *Defender* political cartoon of Booker T. Washington doing the "Buck and Wing" minstrel dance for a white audience.

the relation of the darker races to the lighter races of men."

— W. E. B. Du Bois

offended by what he saw as Washington's surrender. Du Bois stated flatly that it "wasn't enough to teach Negroes trades, the Negro had to have some voice in their government, had to have protection in the courts, and they had to have men to lead them." He believed that the future prosperity of blacks in America lay in men and women like himself — educated African Americans. He coined the term "Talented Tenth" to describe the ten percent of the black population who were educated and relatively affluent. In his famous essay, "The Talented Tenth," Du Bois argued: "Education must not simply teach work — it must teach Life. The Talented Tenth of the Negro race must be made leaders of thought and missionaries of culture among their people."

Many black intellectuals echoed Du Bois's radical sentiment. William Monroe Trotter, founder of Boston's *Guardian* newspaper, and Robert S. Abbott, founder of Chicago's *Defender* paper — both black newspapers — took up the banner of equality in their newspapers and regularly lampooned Booker T. Washington as a puppet of whites.

W. E. B. Du Bois was the leader of the new generation, born free, who believed the only way to win equal rights was to fight for them.

## AUTHENTIC BLACKNESS

WHAT IS BLACK? At the turn of the century blacks were referred to among polite white company as Negroes. But the term was clearly used by whites to mean ignorant, unskilled, rural, and Southern. In short, African Americans were considered all-around inferior. W. E. B. Du Bois and other young African Americans were angered and deeply hurt by this stereotype. They only had to look at themselves to see how wrong that caricature was. They were born free, were educated, and had little connection to the Southern myth of the "Negro." Du Bois himself was a highly educated, Northern-born intellectual who was extremely proud of his accomplishments. As he and his peers looked out at American culture, they saw no representation of their black selves. They argued that it was impossible to make conclusions about African Americans *en masse* because not all blacks look alike or think alike or live alike or even worship alike.

The consequence of the emerging black pride was a tremendous push to act on the dramatic shift in thinking. Blacks began creating their own organizations to free themselves not only from white expectations but also from white control.

**A BLACK WOMAN SPEAKS, 1902**

"I am a colored woman, wife and mother. I have lived all my life in the South,

and have often thought what a peculiar fact it is that the more ignorant the Southern whites

are of us the more vehement they are in their denunciation of us. They boast that they have

little intercourse with us, never see us in our homes, churches or places of amusement,

but still they know us thoroughly."

— Anonymous, New York's *Independent*

A poster for a popular minstrel show around 1900.

## THE MINSTREL MYTH: WHAT BLACK WAS MISTAKEN FOR

At the turn of the century minstrel shows toured every corner of the United States. These shows were comprised primarily of white performers "blacking up" to imitate African Americans. The shows falsely claimed to represent "authentic" blackness, but in reality they merely perpetuated the stereotype of the ignorant, happy-go-lucky, dancing "Nigger" — an extremely demeaning term used primarily by whites to refer to African Americans. The origins of these offensive shows are complex and difficult to untangle, but clearly they resulted from the deep misunderstandings that whites had of blacks. Originally, slaves would mock their masters by performing broad, slapstick imitations of them. They called it "puttin' on ole massa" ("massa" meant "master"). Dances like the "Cake Walk," a formal march in which a black man with a beribboned cane led two couples in a "dignified" strut, and the "Buck and Wing," a classic tap dance step, were created to lampoon white pretensions. When whites witnessed these antics, however, they completely missed the ridicule intended and assumed that these performances were representations of authentic black culture. Whites in turn mocked and ridiculed the supposed naïve and simple-minded ways of black folk for entertainment. The irony of minstrel shows is that whites would put on black faces to imitate blacks imitating whites.

From 1900 to 1905:

- Twenty-eight black-owned banks were formed.
- The National League for the Protection of Colored Women was organized to combat unethical practices by Northern employment agencies.
- The Atlanta Life Insurance Company, the first black insurance business, was founded.
- The National Liberty Party, an all-black national political organization, was formed.
- Numerous African American newspapers, including Boston's *Guardian* and Chicago's *Defender*, were founded.

By virtue of their existence, these organizations and many others exploded the old stereotypes. How could anyone think of African Americans as ignorant Southern laborers when they were running banks and insurance companies, organizing social agencies and political parties, and publishing newspapers across America? Blacks could no longer be limited by class, education, or geography.

## STAND UP, SPEAK OUT!

I N THE WINTER of 1905, Du Bois composed a letter inviting key individuals — teachers, physicians, lawyers, ministers, and a few businessmen — to a meeting to plan action. It was time for the next step in the fight for equal rights.

The original leaders of the Niagara Movement in 1905, in a photo taken on the Canadian side of the Falls, with Du Bois second from right in the second row.

The time seems more than ripe for organized, determined, and aggressive action on the part of men who believe in Negro freedom and growth. Movements are on foot threatening individual freedom and our self respect. I write to you to propose a conference during the coming summer for the following purposes:

I. To oppose firmly the present methods of strangling honest criticism, manipulating public opinion and centralizing political power by means of the improper and corrupt use of money and influence.

II. To organize thoroughly the intelligent and honest Negroes throughout the United States for the purpose of insisting on manhood rights, industrial opportunity and spiritual freedom.

III. To establish and support proper organs of news and public opinion.

If you are in accord with the above objects will you kindly write me at your earliest opportunity as to whether or not you can join the movement indicated in the enclosed circular?

# VIOLENCE'S TEMPORARY TRIUMPH

Between 1889 and 1918, 2,522 blacks were lynched. In many communities, blacks had no legal protection against violence.

Evidence of the Niagara Movement's ineffectuality could be found in the streets across America. Between the years of 1900 and 1909 nearly every attempt by blacks to assert their rights was met by some of the most violent race riots in the nation's history. With the spread of riots to the North, it was clear that racism was no longer just a Southern problem.

## 1900

**NEW ORLEANS**
Race riot erupts and lasts five days. A black school and 30 black homes burned.

**NEW YORK CITY**
Race riot, one black man killed by police. Not a single white arrested.

## 1903

**GEORGIA**
Whites attack blacks in response to a rumor that blacks had murdered whites.

## 1904

**SPRINGFIELD, OH**
A black man shoots and kills a white police officer. Whites break into the jail and lynch him, then destroy the black section of town.

**STATESBORO, GA**
White mob terrorizes blacks. Two men are lynched, two women whipped, and a young mother beaten and killed while her husband is also murdered.

## 1905

**NEW YORK CITY**
Race riot erupts, stemming from police abuse of black citizens.

## 1906

**ATLANTA, GA**
The worst Southern race riot of the decade begins on Saturday, September 24. In the previous weeks the local press had published sensational stories about rapes and murders supposedly committed by blacks, urging the revival of the Ku Klux Klan. On Saturday Atlanta is full of country people who join the mobs in beating and killing countless African Americans and torching their property. The African American president of the Gammon Theological Society is pistol-whipped by a police officer when he asks for help. Seventy people are injured and twelve are killed. The following day W. E. B. Du Bois is on his way to lodge a complaint with the *Atlanta Constitution* newspaper about a lynching. As he passes a butcher shop, he sees the knees of a lynching victim in the window on display with the butchered meat. He never makes it to the newspaper. Instead, he goes home and weeps.

## 1906

**SPRINGFIELD, OH**
Race riot erupts, the second in two years.

**BROWNSVILLE, TX**
Race riot flares up when a group of black soldiers from the segregated 25th Regiment responds to racial insults. Whites go unpunished and President T. Roosevelt dishonorably discharges the entire battalion.

## 1908

**HOUSTON, TX**
Six blacks lynched after being suspected of plotting a murder.

**SPRINGFIELD, IL**
On August 14 and 15, a riot becomes so violent that the governor calls in 4,200 militiamen. The riot had started when the wife of a streetcar conductor falsely claimed that she had been raped by a black man. The mob destroys black businesses and homes, lynches an 84-year-old man, and strings up an innocent barber after burning his shop. No one is ever punished for these crimes. Later, the conductor's wife admits that she had been assaulted by a white man.

**GREENSBURG, IN**
The entire black population is driven from town after a white mob is stopped from lynching a black man convicted of assault.

The response among the Talented Tenth to the letter was enthusiastic. The time for rhetoric had passed, and the time for action was finally here. From July 11 to July 13, 1905, twenty-nine radical black intellectuals from fourteen states met in Fort Erie, Canada, near Niagara Falls. Those present included William Monroe Trotter, editor of the *Guardian,* J. Max Barber, editor of *Voice of the Negro,* and John Hope, president of Atlanta Baptist College. The goal of this group was to fight for African American rights, primarily through the courts, with occasional meetings and an annual convention.

Essentially, they were asking for nothing that had not already been demanded by earlier civil rights organizations. The difference was that this was the first time that members of the Talented Tenth had organized formally as a group. From 1905 to 1909 the group demanded the abolition of all forms of racial discrimination. In addition, the organization called for school integration, voting rights, and the election of blacks to political offices. In the courts, they fought Jim Crow laws, which were established to limit blacks' civil and political rights, and worked to register blacks to vote. They held public meetings in Washington, D.C., Baltimore, New York City, Minneapolis, and Cleveland. Their second convention was held at Harper's Ferry, West Virginia, in 1906 and paid tribute to the martyred John Brown, who tried in 1859 to ignite a violent slave revolt. By these actions the Niagara Movement, as it came to be known, won the support of large numbers of

## Letter to an African-American schoolgirl

In 1905 a teacher wrote to Du Bois asking him to write a letter of encouragement to a student of hers who had become demoralized by white oppression. He obliged.

I wonder if you will let a stranger say a word to you about yourself? I have heard that you are a young woman of some ability but that you are neglecting your schoolwork because you have become hopeless of trying to do anything in the world. I am very sorry for this. How any human whose wonderful fortune it is to live in the 20th Century should under ordinarily fair advantages despair of life is almost unbelievable. And if in addition to this that person is, as I am, of Negro lineage with all the hopes and yearnings of hundreds of millions of human souls dependent in some degree on her striving, then her bitterness amounts to a crime.

There are in the U.S. today tens of thousands of colored girls who would be happy beyond measure to have the chance of educating themselves that you are neglecting. . . . Every time a colored person neglects an opportunity, it makes it more difficult for others of the race to get such an opportunity.

Yours truly,
W. E. B. Du Bois

11

blacks from all over the country.

The importance of the Niagara Movement lay in the fact that it existed at all in the face of Booker T. Washington's opposition and white indifference. Although its more ambitious goals of political and social freedom were not achieved, the movement did give the black community hope that equality was possible. In addition, the movement solidified the Talented Tenth's rejection of Booker T. Washington's stance and provided a platform for African Americans to voice publicly their opposition to racism. Eventually, if blacks continued to protest, loudly and often, whites would have to listen, even if whites found Washington's less-threatening ways much more appealing.

## BIRACIAL STRUGGLE FOR FREEDOM FORMS

**"The Spirit of John Brown Exhibited in Convention at Harpers Ferry. Delegates of the Niagara Movement Make Pilgrimages at Historic Old Building, His Fort, Where they Hold Excercises, and Sing "John Brown's Body" — Demand Equal Rights and Suffrage the Keynote of Speeches and of the Address to the Country Adopted by the Convention."**

Mary Ovington

THIS HEADLINE LED the article written by Mary White Ovington, a white Socialist humanitarian, for the New York *Evening Post* in which she covered the Niagara Movement's Harper's Ferry convention. It was at this convention that Ovington became convinced of its mission's importance. By 1909, however, it was clear to her and other white liberals, as well as the members of the Niagara Movement, that an organization made up solely of blacks could not achieve its goals in such a racist society. The straw that broke the camel's back was the riot in Springfield, Illinois. Not only were blacks and white liberals horrified by the riot itself, but they were also disgusted by the fact that such crimes had spread to the North — and to the home of Abraham Lincoln, no less.

**"We call upon all believers in democracy to join in a national conference and the renewal of the struggle for civil and political liberty."**

The Springfield riot led to a September 3, 1908, article in New York's *Independent* titled "Race War in the South," by William English Walling, a wealthy Southerner and Socialist. In the article, Walling called for a "powerful body of citizens" to assist blacks in their efforts to achieve "absolute and social equality." After reading the article, Mary Ovington wrote Walling in support of his views. This letter led to a meeting in January of 1909, with Walling and Dr. Henry Moskowitz, a white

Lift Every Voice And Sing
(National Negro Hymn)
*Mixed Quartette*

Words by
JAMES WELDON JOHNSON
Class '94

Music by
J. ROSAMOND JOHNSON

Moderato e maestoso

Sop. and Altos

Lift  ev'  ry  voice  and  we
Sto - ny  the  road  we
God  of  our  wea - ry

**LIFT EVERY VOICE**
Black national anthem composed by
James Weldon Johnson and his brother,
J. Rosamund Johnson, first performed
on Lincoln's birthday, February 12, 1900.

New York social worker. Together they decided to issue a call for a meeting on "the Negro question." Oswald Garrison Villard, president of the New York Evening Post Company, was asked to pen the message, which was issued on Lincoln's birthday, February 12, 1909. Prominent black and white activists were asked to sign the document. Fifty-three people put their name to it. In part the announcement read, "We call upon all believers in democracy to join in a national conference and the renewal of the struggle for civil and political liberty."

Between May 31 and June 1 the National Negro Conference met in New York City. Most of the members of the Niagara Movement attended, except for Boston *Guardian* editor William Monroe Trotter, who mistrusted the intentions of white "do-gooders." At the meeting, the attendees voted to incorporate as the National Committee for the Advancement of the Negro Race. In the ensuing months this new organization conducted mass meetings across the country, culminating a year later with another convention in New York. At this conference the group changed its name to the National Association for the Advancement of Colored People (NAACP) and became incorporated as a permanent organization. Like the Niagara Movement, this group was committed to equal civil, political, and education rights; the end of segregation; the right to work; and the protection from violence and intimidation. They criticized the enforcement of the Fourteenth and Fifteenth Amendments to the Constitution, which guarantee Federal protection of civil rights and the right to vote. (Today, the NAACP continues its advocacy for the extension of civil rights into every corner of American society, and it plays an essential role in promoting social and political change.)

The seeds of racial progress were planted in this decade, the first decade of the twentieth century. Without the selfless courage of men and women like W. E. B. Du Bois, William Monroe Trotter, Robert S. Abbot, Mary White Ovington, and many others, African Americans would have remained marginalized and unacknowledged as major contributors to American life and culture.

*The Migrations Series #1*, Jacob Lawrence, 1940-1941.

# MOVING OUT, FIGHTING BACK

**THE GREAT MIGRATION, ORGANIZING FOR FREEDOM, AND WORLD WAR I, 1911–1920**

I pick up my life
And take it away
On a one-way ticket—
Gone up North,
Gone out West,
Gone!

—LANGSTON HUGHES

## GONE UP NORTH!

"Gentlemen, having accepted the position of Director of Publicity and Research in the National Association for the Advancement of Colored People, I hereby place in your hands my resignation," wrote W. E. B. Du Bois on July 5, 1910, when he resigned his professorship at Atlanta University. With this action, Du Bois packed his bags and moved his family to New York City. His migration North not only helped define the NAACP's mission, but it also provided an early indication of what was to come in the decade that has been described as the years of the Great Migration.

At the beginning of the decade the NAACP wavered between two possible missions. The first was that it would be an organization run and financed by whites. As such, it would be dedicated to uplifting the civil rights of African Americans. The second option emphasized the interracial quality of the organization. In this vision, people from both sides of the race line would work together to ensure that every citizen, including the nation's historic minority, claimed equal rights. As Director of Publicity and Research, Du Bois quickly became the voice of the NAACP. What he said was what the organization stood for. When he set up his office in the *Evening Post* building in lower Manhattan rather than Harlem, Du Bois made it clear to everyone that the NAACP's mission was one of interracial cooperation and an activist agenda.

Du Bois brought out the first issue of the NAACP's monthly magazine, the *Crisis,* on November 1, 1910. In future issues Du Bois intended to highlight the dangers of racial prejudice and support the rights of all people, regardless of race. The *Crisis*'s first editorial spelled this out:

> **[The NAACP] stand[s] for rights of men, irrespective of color or race, for the highest ideals of American democracy, and for reasonable but earnest and persistent attempts to gain these rights and realize their ideals.**

Only 1,000 copies of the first issue of the *Crisis* were printed. Nevertheless, Du Bois was energized, finally having a forum that appeared regularly to publish his beliefs. He did not waste any time in creating a strong and forceful voice against oppression. By the March issue, the *Crisis* had become the voice that boldly identified the most pressing civil rights issues — most prominently segregation. "This discriminatory practice arose in three forms: attempts at residential segregation through property-holders' covenants; efforts toward that end through mob violence; and legislation to force Negroes to live in restricted areas."

By 1918, the *Crisis* would be publishing more than 100,000 copies of each issue and would become one of the most influential black publications in the nation.

An NAACP recruitment poster.

1920 *Crisis* political cartoon — "The Reason"

## MOVING FEVER

WHEN THE NAACP established its main office in the North, no one was surprised. The organization could not have survived in the South, where whites used all means — legal and illegal — to suppress independent black voices. The NAACP was not alone, however, in realizing that the North offered blacks wider freedoms than the South. Thousands upon thousands of African Americans took to trains, broken-down trucks, old jalopies with bald tires, and whatever else would take them North.

Following the NAACP's lead, the National League on Urban Conditions Among Negroes, another interracial organization, was formed in 1910 by the merger of three New York–based organizations: the Committee on Urban Conditions Among Negroes, the National League for the Protection of Colored Women, and the Committee for the Improvement of Industrial Conditions Among Negroes in New York. The National Urban League, as it was renamed in 1920, sought to improve the working and living conditions of urban blacks as well as to broaden employment opportunities. The League trained social workers and fought to change housing, health, sanitation, recreation, and employment conditions. The organization was spurred into existence by the abuses that Southern blacks, particularly young black women, encountered by unscrupulous whites who essentially enslaved these newcomers.

The NAACP's first legal victory was won in 1915 when the Supreme Court declared that "grandfather clauses" in the Oklahoma and Maryland State Constitutions violated the Fifteenth Amendment and were, therefore, null and void. "Grandfather clauses" restricted voting to those who were descendants of persons who had voted prior to 1866. Of course, no blacks voted before 1866.

The attempts of the National Urban League, the NAACP, and other organizations to improve life and work conditions of blacks in Northern cities did not go unnoticed in the South. In fact, there was a steady stream of letters and newspaper articles arriving all over the South from Northerners testifying to the possibility of a better life. However, no one idealized life in the North as perfect. The more common view was one of a clear-eyed assessment of the degrees of bad, a feeling that W. E. B. Du Bois summarized:

**"The North is no paradise, but the South is at best a system of caste and insult and, at worst, a hell."**

17

Fed up with the racism and oppression they experienced daily, blacks all over the South were tantalized by the stories they heard about Northern blacks riding street cars and attending theaters and amusement parks without Jim Crow segregation. One black man who had migrated to Philadelphia wrote home:

> I don't have to "master" every little boy comes along. . . . Since being in the state of Pa I can ride in the electric street and steam cars where I get a seat.

A carpenter who moved to Chicago wrote home to Mississippi:

> I was promoted on the first of the month. I should have been here 20 years ago. I just began to feel like a man. My children are going to the same school with whites and I don't have to umble to no one. I have registered, will vote the next election and there isn't any 'yes sir' and 'no sir' — its all yea and no and Sam and Bill.

## A NEW KIND OF SLAVERY

A common practice among employment agencies hiring domestic workers was to make them sign a contract that made it nearly impossible to leave a job, no matter how awful the working conditions. To break the contract meant losing everything the worker owned. The following is a contract from a domestic help agency in Richmond, Virginia.

Family arriving from the South.

In consideration of my expenses being paid from Richmond to __Philadelphia__ and a situation provided for me, I agree to give __two years__ services after arrival as __a maid__ to party or persons paying my expenses. And I further agree that all my personal effects may be subject to their order until I have fulfilled that contract, forfeiting all claims to said personal effects after sixty days after this date should I fail to comply with agreement.

"Every time a lynching takes place in a community down South, you can depend on it that colored people will arrive in Chicago within two weeks."

— Chicago's Urban League President T. Arnold Hall

**1916 WORK SONG**

Boll-weevil in de cotton

Cut worm in de cotton,

Devil in de white man,

Wah's goin' on.

The promise of a better life was not the only driving force behind the migration north. In 1915 and 1916, two natural disasters provided deadly blows to the Southern agricultural economy. First, there was a drought, which was followed by rains and floods. Next, a record boll weevil infestation decimated the crops, leaving black laborers and sharecroppers without a harvest two years in a row. These disasters, combined with the racial climate of the South, made it almost impossible for blacks to survive. News from the North, however, was glowing.

One other development was key to inciting the Great Migration — the sharp decrease in European immigrants as a result of World War I. When the war began in 1914, immigrants arriving from Europe numbered 1,218,480. By the next year, the numbers dropped to 326,700, and by 1918, only 110,618 immigrants entered the United States from Europe. This plunge in a large white, unskilled labor force made northern industry desperate for workers. The desperation was doubled when America entered the war in 1917 and four million Americans were conscripted for military service.

**WANTED:**

Men for laborers and semi-skilled occupation. Address or apply to employment department.

**Westinghouse Electric & Manufacturing Co.**

From late 1915 onward, recruiting agents for northern industry traveled to the South for laborers. They would offer free railroad tickets or advance the tickets against future wages. Sometimes, trains would just back into small towns and steam away with nearly the entire black population. The jobs being offered up north paid considerably more than those in the South. In the North, the average wage for black workers was between $3.00 and $3.60 per day; steelworkers earned up to $4.50 a day. In the South, black steelworkers in Birmingham, Alabama, made just $2.50 for a back-breaking nine-hour day, and only four percent of all Southern black workers broke the $3.00-a-day ceiling. By 1920, at least 300,000 — possibly many more — African-American farmers, unskilled laborers, and domestics had left the South.

19

Letters sent to the Chicago *Defender* requesting information on job opportunities:

Sir:
I would thank you kindly to explain to me how you get work and what term I am comeing to Chicago this spring and would like to know jest what to do would thank and appreciate a letter from you soon telling me the thing that I wont to know.
— a man from Atlanta, Georgia

I saw an advertisement in the Chicago Ledger where you would send tickets to any one desireing to come up there. I am a married man with a wife only, I am 38 years of age, and both of us have so far splendid health, and would like very much to come out there provided we could get good employment regarding the advertisement.
— a man from Savannah, Georgia

## THE BEST AND THE BRIGHTEST GO NORTH!

W. E. B. DU BOIS was not the only prominent black to move North. After nearly a decade of self-imposed exile in Nicaragua and Venezuela working for the U.S. Consulate, James Weldon Johnson returned to the United States in 1914 and joined the editorial staff at the *New York Age*. An acclaimed composer, poet, novelist, journalist, and diplomat, Johnson was one of the most respected African Americans in the country. In addition to having composed the black national anthem "Lift Every Voice," he had published anonymously in 1912 one of the first modern African-American novels, *The Autobiography of an Ex-Colored Man*. His move to New York underscored the change in attitude among African Americans from one of despair to one of hope. Now, it was possible to make a livable wage and go about

## PERCENTAGE OF AFRICAN-AMERICAN POPULATION INCREASE IN MAJOR NORTHERN CITIES FROM 1910 TO 1920

DETROIT _____ +611.3%

CHICAGO _____ +148.2%

COLUMBUS, OH _____ +74%

NEW YORK CITY ____ +66.3%

INDIANAPOLIS ___ +59%

CINCINNATTI ___ +53.2%

PITTSBURGH __ +47.2%

one's business without the constant threat of violence and overt racism. In the next six years Johnson would become a major player in the NAACP. First, in 1916, he would become field secretary, and four years later he woud be named the first African-American secretary of the organization. As secretary, Johnson became the chief operating officer and, along with Du Bois, the most influential African American fighting for civil rights.

James Weldon Johnson

Other prominent African Americans also arrived in the North in the early years of the decade. Madam C. J. Walker had founded one of the most successful black businesses in St. Louis, Missouri, but she moved her family and her business to New York, where she could enjoy her success and support organizations like the NAACP more directly. Around the same time, poet Claude McKay left his native Jamaica to become one of the first black editors on a white magazine, the *Liberator*. In addition, musician, songwriter, and publisher W. C. Handy left Memphis to open one of the first black-owned recording companies, Black Swan. Essentially, any African American who desired a better life and greater opportunity moved North.

## BLACK MOSES

THREE YEARS AFTER Johnson returned to the United States, Marcus Garvey emigrated from Jamaica. He was hailed as the "Black Moses" and eventually led the largest organized mass movement in African-American history. Now Garvey is remembered primarily as the creator and most vocal proponent of the back-to-Africa movement that swept the world after World War I. He galvanized his race in a program of self-help and African nationalism through his Universal Negro Improvement Association (UNIA). At its height UNIA had six million members, published the largest black weekly newspaper — *Negro World* — created a myriad of black self-help institutions, and ran numerous businesses. Marcus Garvey proclaimed in a speech:

### AUTOBIOGRAPHY OF AN EX-COLORED MAN
### by James Weldon Johnson

*The novel examines how impossible it is to live as a black man in a white American culture. The narrator's white benefactor spells this out by urging the biracial narrator to pass for white, since he is not the stereotypically ignorant, Southern black laborer and, thus, cannot really be black.*

My boy, you are by blood, by appearance, by education, and by tastes a white man. Now why do you want to throw your life away amidst poverty and ignorance, in the hopeless struggle, of the black people in the United States? . . . This idea of you making a Negro of yourself is nothing more than a sentiment, and you do not realize the fearful import of what you intend to do. What kind of Negro would you make now, especially in the South?

The time has come for the Negro to forget and cast behind him his hero worship and adoration of the other races, and to start out immediately to create and emulate heroes of his own. We must canonize our own martyrs, and elevate to positions of fame and honor black men and women who have made their distinct contributions to our racial history.

Marcus Garvey

In contrast to Du Bois, who focused on the Talented Tenth, Garvey spoke to the "untalented ninetieth," offering them hope for a better life. The Reverend Adam E. Clayton Powell Sr., pastor of the Abyssinian Baptist Church, was not a follower of Marcus Garvey, but he understood Garvey's importance:

The coming of Marcus Garvey to Harlem in 1916 was more significant to the Negro than the World War, the southern exodus and the fluctuation of property values up- and down-town. Garvey, with his Black United States, Black President and Black Vice President, Black Cabinet, Black Congress, Black Army with Black Generals, Black Cross Nurses, Black Negro World, Black Star Line and a Black Religion with a Black God, had awakened a race-consciousness that made Harlem felt around the world. The cotton picker of Alabama, bending over his basket, and the poor ignorant Negro of the Mississippi Delta, crushed beneath a load of prejudice, lifted their heads and said, "Let's go to Harlem to see this Black Moses. . . . [H]e is the only man that ever made Negroes who are black not ashamed of their color.

Not everyone admired Garvey, however. In fact, many prominent members of the Talented Tenth despised him. Ever-conscious of how the white world viewed them, they were offended by UNIA's extravagant uniforms and the elaborate titles awarded its members, which to them seemed suggestive of minstrel shows. Garvey and his followers, however, were not concerned with how whites perceived them. Their mission was to uplift the race, not to make whites feel better about blacks. One important aspect of this mission was pride and self-respect. The uniforms, parades, and titles were effective tools in achieving these goals.

"The time has come for the Negro to forget and cast behind him his hero worship and adoration of the other races."

UNIA member in full uniform.

# THE SINKING OF MARCUS GARVEY

PART OF GARVEY's plan was to establish in Africa a nation of descendants of slaves. In 1919, he founded a shipping line called the Black Star Line to take African Americans back to Africa as well as allow black people on either side of the Atlantic to exchange goods and services. From its inception, this shipping line created enormous publicity, but Garvey's experience with running such a complex business was minimal. Quickly, the line was overwhelmed by financial obligations and mismanagement, causing it to fail before a voyage was ever completed.

With support from the NAACP, the United States government indicted Garvey on charges of mail fraud stemming from Garvey's stock promotion of the Black Star Line. The pressure from this indictment pushed Garvey into a fatal mistake. In June of 1922, Edward Young Clarke, the acting imperial wizard of the Ku Klux Klan in Atlanta, Georgia, sought out and offered Garvey and his organization financing help, exploiting the Klan's desire to rid America of blacks. When news of this meeting became public, outrage was almost universal among blacks. Thus, Garvey's fate was sealed. His subsequent conviction on the mail fraud charges only hastened the inevitable. After spending thirty-three months in federal prison, Garvey was deported to Jamaica and never allowed to return to America.

Black Star Line ship, *Frederick Douglass.*

## PATRIOTISM NOW, JUSTICE LATER

JUST WHEN IT looked as if blacks were making real progress toward equal rights, the United States went to war. In April 1917, the country entered World War I under the banner "Make the World Safe for Democracy." Blacks responded bitterly to the implication that America was already "Safe for Democracy." The thirty-eight blacks who were lynched the previous year offered real evidence to the contrary. Nevertheless, African Americans responded so strongly to the call to serve that, after initial reluctance, the U.S. Army formed two black divisions, the Ninety-second and the Ninety-third.

This surge of patriotism might seem surprising, but it was perhaps felt strongest by black leaders, who believed that this was the African American's chance to prove his worth. To encourage black participation in and support of the war effort, a number of prominent African Americans came out in support of the war. No black was more vocal in his or her support than W. E. B. Du Bois, and he wrote a number of editorials in the *Crisis* to express his point of view.

**Excerpt from "Close Ranks"**
**an editorial written by W. E. B. Du Bois in the *Crisis***

This is the crisis of the world. For all the long years to come men will point to the year 1918 as the great Day of Decision. . . . We of the colored race have no ordinary interest in the outcome. That which the German power represents today spells death to the aspirations of Negroes and all the darker races for equality, freedom, and democracy. Let us not hesitate. Let us, while this war lasts, forget our special grievances and close our ranks shoulder to shoulder with our white fellow citizens and the allied nations that are fighting for democracy. We make no ordinary sacrifice, but we make it gladly and willingly with our eyes lifted to the hills.

While blacks displayed enormous patriotism and courage, the response by the white majority was not equally enthusiastic. Southern whites were all for drafting blacks, but they were clearly against training them in their own backyard. Repeatedly, black regiments faced discrimination and hostility in Southern towns. In Camp Greene, North Carolina, YMCA canteens excluded black troops, while whites in Spartanburg, South Carolina, attacked Sergeant Noble Sissle of the 15th New York Infantry. (Sissle later became an acclaimed jazz singer, composer, and conductor.) A riot by black soldiers in response to the attack was avoided only by transplanting the troops to Europe earlier than planned.

The most serious riot involving black troops since the Brownsville riot a decade earlier broke out in Houston, Texas, on August 23, 1917. It began when two police officers trying to arrest a black woman beat and incarcerated a black soldier when he tried to intervene. A rumor that a second soldier had been shot and killed by white police quickly circulated the military base. In retaliation, more than 100 armed black soldiers from the 24th

Infantry Division marched on the city. Conflicting accounts of the death toll range from thirteen to forty.

African Americans punished:

- 156 black soldiers court-martialed on the charge of mutiny
- 41 sentenced to life in prison
- 13 hanged immediately without appeal
- 6 more executed later

Whites punished: None.

**"The Negroes of the entire country will regard the 13 Negro soldiers of the Twenty-fourth Infantry executed as martyrs."**

—Baltimore *Afro-American*

## TOO MANY DEAD

WHILE AFRICAN-AMERICAN soldiers struggled against racism in the military, the black population in the rest of the country fared no better. With the intense labor shortage, African Americans were recruited by Northern industries as never before. At the same time, the arrival of cheap black labor angered the white workers who were organizing labor unions to bargain for better wages and working conditions. The newly arrived black workers threatened their livelihood. Industrialists took advantage of this natural conflict to crush unionizing efforts in their factories. The consequences, however, were grave.

As a result of industrial and railroad companies importing thousands of black laborers into East St. Louis, Illinois, one of the worst riots in U.S. history ignited. Over three days from July 1 to July 3, 1917, more than 200 blacks and 8 whites were killed, and 6,000 blacks were burned out of their homes. Because the damage was so extensive and many blacks fled the city and never returned, it will never be known exactly how many people were killed in that riot. Some estimates suggest at least 2,000 blacks were murdered.

Antilynching flag outside the NAACP offices in New York City.

25

## WHY WE MARCH

We march because by the grace of God and the force of truth the dangerous, hampering walls of prejudice and inhuman injustices must fall.

We march because we want to make impossible a repetition of Waco, Memphis, and East St. Louis by arousing the conscience of the country, and to bring the murderers of our brothers, sisters, and innocent children to justice.

We march because we are thoroughly opposed to Jim Crow cars, segregation, discrimination, disfranchisement, lynching, and the host of evils that are forced on us. It is time that the spirit of Christ should be manifested in the making and execution of laws.

We march because we want our children to live in a better land and enjoy fairer conditions than have fallen to our lot.

Leaflet handed out at the Silent Protest Parade protesting lynching and discrimination.

Despite their desire to keep African Americans supporting the government and the war effort, W. E. B. Du Bois, James Weldon Johnson, and the officers of the NAACP could not remain passive in their response to the East St. Louis riot. On July 28, 1917, a little more than three weeks after the riot had ended, the NAACP organized a silent march. Between 10,000 and 15,000 blacks silently marched down Fifth Avenue in New York City to protest continued lynchings and discrimination in the South and elsewhere. The march not only alerted whites that blacks would no longer stand for racism but also showed fellow African Americans that black leaders could simultaneously support the war and protest injustice within the nation's borders. The Silent Protest Parade, as it came to be known, was a success and was the first nonviolent mass protest by blacks. It would set the stage for the civil rights movement three decades later.

# HEROES MARCH HOME TO THE "RED SUMMER"

**D**ESPITE THEIR CONFLICTING feelings of patriotism and bitterness, many
African Americans did more than simply step forward to serve in the war. They
served above and beyond the call of duty. Of the 400,000 enlisted African-
American soldiers, 200,000 served in Europe, and more than 50,000 fought on the front
lines. The regimental motto of the 367th Infantry was "See It Through." A steadiness and
determination in the battlefield characterized all black soldiers who saw action. The 370th
Infantry won twenty-one American Distinguished Service Crosses and sixty-eight French
War Crosses. The entire 369th Infantry, the first black troops to see action, were awarded
the Croix de Guerre for gallantry in battle for holding the line under continuous fire for
a record-breaking 191 days. This remarkable feat led the French High Command to give
the 369th its supreme mark of honor by choosing the regiment to lead all Allied forces into
the Rhine. This infantry was also nicknamed the "Hell Fighters" by the French.

The admiration that African-American soldiers earned from the French was not
shared by the military commanders of their own country. In fact, the U.S. War
Department worked to downplay black achievements and encouraged the French to do

African-
American U.S.
Army infantry
troops march-
ing northwest
of Verdun,
France.

25042

the same. A secret document created by the American high command in August of 1918 was sent to the "French Military Mission Stationed with the American Army." The memorandum, titled "Secret Information Concerning the Black American Troops," warned of the dangers of treating black soldiers as equals:

> I. We must prevent the rise of any pronounced degree of intimacy of French officers and black officers. We may be courteous and amiable with the last, but we cannot deal with them on the same plane as with the white American officer without deeply wounding the latter. We must not eat with them, must not shake hands or seek to talk or meet with them outside of the requirements of military service.
>
> II. We must not commend too highly the [black] American troops, particularly in the presence of [white] Americans. . . .
>
> III. Make a point of keeping the native [civilian] population from spoiling the Negroes. [White] Americans become greatly incensed at any public expression of intimacy between white women and black men.

The War Department and many whites back home had reason to fear the return of well-trained African-American soldiers fresh from the success of battle against the fierce German army. Not only were these men confident of their abilities but they were also trained to fight back against aggression. Despite reservations by many whites across the nation, when the men of the Fifteenth Regiment of the New York National Guard marched home to Harlem on a clear February morning in 1919, thousands of blacks and whites lined Fifth Avenue to celebrate their bravery. In the *New York Age*, James Weldon Johnson described the event:

> The Fifteenth furnished the first sight that New York has had of seasoned soldiers in marching order. There was no militia smartness about their appearance; their 'tin

## AMERICA'S FIRST HERO

The first American soldier in World War I to receive the Croix de Guerre with star and palm was Sergeant Henry Johnson from Albany, New York. The battle in which he fought became known as the "Battle of Henry Johnson." On May 14, 1918, Johnson was on outpost guard duty with Private Needham Roberts when a raiding party of twenty Germans attacked. Both Johnson and Needham were wounded. After Johnson had fired his last bullet, he attacked the Germans with the butt end of his rifle and a bolo knife to free Roberts. Together, Johnson and Roberts killed four Germans, wounded several more, and held their post as the rest fled.

hats' were battered and rusty and the shiny newness worn off their bayonets, but they were men who had gone through the terrible hell of war and come back.

The sense in the community was that African Americans, newly empowered, were at the beginning of a new age of freedom and justice. In his editorial in the *Crisis,* Du Bois wrote:

> The faults of *our* country are our faults. Under similar circumstances, we would fight again. But by the God of heaven, we are cowards and jackasses if now that the war is over we do not marshal every ounce of our brain and brawn to fight a sterner, longer, more unbending battle against the forces of hell in our own land.
> *We return.*
> *We return from fighting.*
> *We return fighting.*
> Make way for democracy! We saved it in France, and by the Great Jehovah, we will save it in the United States of America, or know the reason why.

Unfortunately, this optimism was short-lived. By summertime, white retaliation was in full swing. Over the next seven months more than twenty-five major race riots would occur across the nation and eighty-three African Americans would be lynched. The Ku Klux Klan, revived in 1916, would hold more than 200 meetings from Indiana to New England to Florida. In disgust, James Weldon Johnson dubbed the summer of 1919 the "Red Summer" in response to all the blood that was spilled.

*Doughboy,* Edward Arlington Harrison, *circa* 1926.

**"These boys have been fine soldiers here, and if they ever get back from France, I'm big enough to lick any man who don't give 'em a square deal."**

— An African-American Sergeant from the 371st Infantry Regiment, upon leaving Camp Jackson, South Carolina

29

**MAY 10, 1919  CHARLESTON, SOUTH CAROLINA**
A white sailor shoots an African-American civilian to death. Unlike the other 25 race riots that occurred this year, Charleston officials with the help of the Marines restore order overnight with only two blacks killed and seventeen wounded; seven sailors and one policeman are injured.

**JUNE, 1919  ELLISVILLE, MISSISSIPPI**
A white mob fatally wounds an alleged rapist named John Hartfield as he flees through a cane field. A local doctor keeps Hartfield alive for the lynching the next day. Town newspapers announce the time and place. Three thousand people gather at the appointed tree. Hartfield is hanged, burned, and shot. Governor Theodore Bilbo refuses to stop the action, saying, "Nobody can keep the inevitable from happening."

**JULY, 1919  LONGVIEW, TEXAS**
The National Negro Business League chapter in town persuades black farmers to bypass the local white growers and negotiate directly with buyers in Galveston. The body of a young African-American man is found outside town stripped nude and shot dead; the latest issue of the Chicago *Defender* arrives in town with a detailed account of the murder. White townspeople quickly conclude that a local African-American teacher and doctor are the authors of the article. On July 10, both men are beaten and ordered to leave town by sundown. The two men defy the order. When a mob gathers in front of the doctor's house, more than 150 shots are fired. At least one black and four whites are killed and many are wounded. Order is restored finally by the state militia and Texas rangers after a number of houses are burned and the doctor's father is savagely murdered.

**JULY, 1919  WASHINGTON, D.C.**
Spurred on by the *Washington Post*, a white mob is encouraged to "clean up" the city by ridding it of blacks. Like in Longview, blacks fight back. When the Secretary of War finally orders 2,000 infantry to restore order, more than 100 people have been injured and 6 have been killed.

**JULY, 1919  CHICAGO, ILLINOIS**
For five days blacks and whites fight back and forth across Wentworth Avenue, the street dividing the white blue-collar stockyard neighborhoods from the Black Belt. When the riot ends, 15 whites and 23 blacks are dead, 537 people are wounded, and more than 1,000 are homeless.

Poet Claude McKay memorialized the bloody season
of 1919 in the following poem, which was published
later that year in the white magazine *Liberator*.

### IF WE MUST DIE

If we must die, let it not be like hogs
Hunted and penned in the inglorious spot,
While round us bark the mad and hungry dogs,
Making their mock at our accursed lot.
If we must die, O let us nobly die,
So that our precious blood may not be shed
In Vain; then even the monsters we defy
Shall be constrained to honor us though dead!
O kinsmen! We must meet the common foe!
Though far outnumbered let us show us brave,
And for their thousand blows deal one deathblow!
What though before us lies the open grave?
Like men we'll face the murderous, cowardly pack,
Pressed to the wall, dying, but fighting back!

—CLAUDE MCKAY

Armistice Day at Lenox Ave. and 134th St., 1919.

# BLACK METROPOLIS

**THE RISE OF HARLEM, 1900–1920**

### HARLEM WINE

This is not water running here,
These thick rebellious streams
That hurtle flesh and bone past fear
Down alleyways of dreams.

This is a wine that must flow on
Not caring how or where,
So it has ways to flow upon
Where song is in the air.

So it can woo an artful flute
With loose, elastic lips,
Its measurements of joy compute
With blithe, ecstatic hips.

— COUNTEE CULLEN

## BLACK BOHEMIA

BY THE TIME W. E. B. Du Bois moved to Harlem in 1911, and James Weldon Johnson followed in 1914, Harlem was a neighborhood in bold transition. The neighborhood above 110th Street in Manhattan was far from the sleepy white upper-class enclave it was at the turn of the century. Yet Harlem was also a long way from the throbbing black metropolis it was destined to become.

In 1911, the center of black life was still downtown in a section of Manhattan called Black Bohemia. Ranging from Twenty-seventh to Fifty-third Streets on the West Side of Manhattan, Black Bohemia was little more than a ghetto. The streets were tightly packed with boarding houses and tenements. The streets and sidewalks were choked with wagons and pedestrians.

## BLACK MAIN STREET, *CIRCA* 1900–1910

West Fifty-third Street between Sixth and Seventh Avenues was black New York's main street. Almost all of the community's major institutions were located here: political clubs, Mount Olivet Baptist Church, St. Marks Methodist Episcopal Church, St. Benedict the Moor Roman Catholic Church, the major black fraternal societies, two black hotels, the Negro YMCA, and the offices of many of the 42 black physicians and 26 black lawyers who serviced the 60,000 African Americans of New York City.

At this time the average black worker earned about seven dollars a week. A tiny four-room apartment in Black Bohemia rented for twenty dollars a month, about two to five dollars more than in white neighborhoods. Obviously, this left little for a family to live on. To make matters worse, Black Bohemia had become the location of the city's brothels and gambling dens. White landlords preferred these "sporting life" tenants because they demanded fewer, if any, improvements than respectable workers, and they were willing to pay even higher rents. By the second decade of the century, rent gouging in Black Bohemia had reached such a crisis that it had become the butt of jokes by black comedians and was featured in a classic black vaudeville song: "Rufus Johnson Brown, what you gwine do when de rent comes roun'?"

Harlem, by contrast, was a paradise of almost unimaginable splendor. Whatever it took to escape the squalor of midtown Manhattan was worth the sacrifice for blacks. The name "Harlem" evoked ele-

♪♪ "Now I started at the bottom, and I stays right there,

Black tenement homes in the San Juan Hill district, in the West 60s; subway construction, Lenox Ave. and 113th St., 1901.

34

gance and distinction. Its streets and avenues were broad, well paved, and tree-lined, and its buildings were aristocratic apartment houses and beautiful brownstone homes — "finished in high-style," as one turn-of-the-century advertisement trumpeted. This was a far cry from Black Bohemia's claustrophobic, windowless tenements.

Harlem earned its grand reputation in the 1880s and 1890s, when developers envisioned this sanctuary on the northern edge of Manhattan as a white, upper-class haven from the bustle and clatter of downtown. In 1880 the elevated railroad was built along Eighth Avenue. This mass transportation opened up the west side of Harlem. Next, the subway was scheduled to be built under Lenox Avenue on the East Side by 1904. With subway trains traveling at forty miles per hour, the eight-mile ride to City Hall became a matter of minutes instead of hours on a streetcar. This news caused a sudden development boom. Speculators invested an enormous amount of capital in Harlem, and real estate values skyrocketed as investors anticipated huge profits. These investors could just imagine thousands of white, upper-middle class commuters unloading from the new subway stations. Unfortunately, too many developers believed the same thing. Harlem quickly became overbuilt years before the completion date of the new subway. By 1902 whole buildings remained unoccupied as they waited for the expected flood of tenants, which would not come for another two years. Facing financial ruin, developers went begging for tenants. At dire times like these, economic necessity can override racial prejudice.

**October 27, 1904**
The Interborough Rapid Transit subway system was completed to 148th Street and Lenox Avenue. The fare was five cents.

don't seem like I'm gonna get nowhere." ♫

— lyrics from a blues song

Designed by famous architect Stanford White, Strivers Row, on 138th and 139th Streets between Seventh and Eighth Avenues, contained some of the finest apartments and homes in New York City.

## INVASION OF HARLEM

W HILE BLACK BOHEMIA in midtown was bursting well beyond its capacity, a young twenty-four-year-old African American named Philip A. Payton Jr. recognized just how desperate the white owners of empty apartment buildings up in Harlem really were. In 1903 Payton negotiated a deal with the white landlords to lease a few houses on West 134th Street, east of Lenox Avenue. He knew that middle-class blacks would pay almost anything to get out of the overcrowded, crumbling tenements of midtown, so he offered landlords a rental rate above the depressed real estate price. Then he added a percentage to the rent for himself and was still able to offer apartments that seemed reasonable when compared with the high rents of Black Bohemia.

In a 1912 interview, Payton described how the deal came about:

> I was a real estate agent, making a specialty in management of colored tenement property for nearly a year before I actually succeeded in getting a colored tenement to manage. My first opportunity came as a result of a dispute between two landlords in West 134th Street. To 'get even' one of them turned his house over to me to fill with colored tenants. I was successful in renting and managing this house, after a time I was able to induce other landlords to . . . give me their houses to manage.

A black family moves into Harlem, about 1905. The apartments in this building are advertised as "For Respectable Colored Families Only."

> "It is no longer necessary for our people to live in small, dingy, stuffy apartments."
>
> —*New York Age*, 1906

With that first foot in the door, Payton was able to expand the number of properties he managed, first to the west and then across Lenox Avenue. Neither Payton nor the white property owners could have seen what was to come — the wholesale migration of blacks from downtown Manhattan to Harlem. Nor could Payton have imagined the extent of the outrage of whites over a few black families' moving into that segregated community.

**A newspaper article from the *New York Herald*, December 24, 1905**

## NEGROES MOVE INTO HARLEM

An untoward circumstance has been injected into the private-dwelling market in the vicinity of 133rd and 134th Streets. During the last three years the flats in 134th Street between Lenox and Seventh Avenues, that were occupied entirely by white folks, have been captured for occupation by a Negro population. Its presence there has tended also to lend much color to conditions in 133rd and 135th Streets between Lenox and Seventh Avenues.

One Hundred and Thirty-third Street still shows some signs of resistance to the blending of colors in that street, but between Lenox and Seventh Avenues has practically succumbed to the ingress of colored tenants. Nearly all the old dwellings in 134th Street to midway in the block west of Seventh Avenue are occupied by colored tenants, and real estate brokers predict that it is only a matter of time when the entire block, to Eighth Avenue, will be a stronghold of the Negro population.

As a result of the extension of this African colony dwellings in 133rd Street between Seventh and Eighth Avenues, and in 132nd Street from Lenox to Eighth Avenues, have depreciated from fifteen to twenty per cent in value, especially in the sides of those streets nearest to 134th Street. The cause of the colored influx is inexplicable.

=== ORIGIN ===

OF THE

**Afro-American Realty Company**

THE Afro-American Realty Company recently incorporated under the laws of the State of New York for $500,000 to operate in New York City Real Estate, had its origin in ten men, who over a year ago, joined themselves together, into co-partnership for the above mentioned purpose. They began by taking five year leases on flat houses and renting them to people of their own race. The success that met their efforts by far exceeded the expectation of the most optimistic of the co-partnership. In less than six months they were in control of ten flat houses, with an earning capacity of over $5,000 per annum.

**Prejudice of White Owner and Agent Cause of Present Condition.**

The reason for the present condition of the colored tenancy in New York City to-day, is because of the race prejudice of the white owner and his white agent. When the owner becomes colored and his agent colored, then there is compelled to come an improvement of the condition.

**Race Prejudice Turned into Dollars and Cents.**

Race prejudice is a luxury and like all other luxuries, can be made very expensive in New York City, if the Negroes will but answer this call of the Afro-American Realty Company. With a cash capital of $500,000, the Afro-American Realty Company can turn race prejudice into dollars and cents. The very prejudice which has heretofore worked against us can be turned and used to our profit.

## THE REAL ESTATE WAR

AS AFRICAN AMERICANS increasingly found more apartments available, white residents became fearful their neighborhoods would soon be "overrun" by blacks. As a result they organized to choke off the black expansion by forming holding companies to buy the properties adjacent to the black apartment buildings. Likewise, the Hudson Realty Company was created with one mission: to purchase buildings that housed blacks and then to evict them. An organization called the Property Owners Protective Association incorporated another real estate company "to get rid of colored people" and to "prevent Negroes from coming to Harlem to live." Their president, John G. Taylor, told the *Harlem Home News* that they would work to make it "impossible for white renegades to borrow any more money for the purpose of backing Negro speculators in their value-destroying ventures."

**"Race prejudice is a luxury and like all other luxuries, can be made very expensive in New York City..."**

Outraged, blacks fought this white resistance every way they could. Payton organized the Afro-American Realty Company, capitalized at $500,000 ($9,085,000 in today's dollars) to buy and lease houses to rent to African-American tenants. Others made it a point of racial pride to buy Harlem property, dispossess whites, and install members of their own race. Influential African Americans in the press and in the church urged people to buy and lease in Harlem to drive the racists out.

Still, the whites fought hard to exclude blacks. The *New York Indicator,* a real estate publication, spoke of the "invasion" of Harlem and suggested that the only fit place for blacks to live was "in some colony in the outskirts of the city, where their transportation and other problems will not inflict injustice and disgust on worthy citizens."

In 1913 white politicians of Harlem attempted to build a playground on the side of the 18th-century Watt Mansion to encourage white residents to stay. By 1914, however, the mansion had become the location of the Libya Hotel, the first black nightclub in Harlem.

The WATT ESTATE—An Entire City Block
From Lenox to Seventh Avenues, 139th to 140th Streets

THE PINCKNEY HOMESTEAD

## A Natural Playground Site in the Heart of Harlem

Endorsed by City Officials, The Harlem Board of Commerce, The Boys' and Girls' "Get-What-You-Want" Club and others, as one of Harlem's most needed public improvements.

¶ If you want the City to acquire this property for a play ground, *NOW* is the time to act.—Write to the Mayor, Presidents of the Borough and Board of Alderman, how badly you need this playground for your children.

Right, an advertisement to turn the Watt Mansion in Harlem into a white haven. Below, the interior of the Watt Mansion in 1913 after it became the Lybia, Harlem's first black club.

"If you want the City to acquire this property for a play ground, NOW is the time to act."

39

## WHITE FLIGHT

THE PRESSURE APPLIED on the Afro-American Realty Company by such organizations as Property Owners Protective Association made it impossible for the company to survive. The company could not acquire mortgages from banks, and the leases it did have were canceled; the company's capital alone was not nearly enough to keep it above water. Enraged by the company's failure, Philip A. Payton Jr. tried to give white Harlem residents a taste of their own medicine. He entered into a partnership with J. C. Thomas, a prosperous black undertaker, to buy two five-story apartment houses, evict the whites, and rent the apartments to black tenants. Another real estate firm was also formed by two salesmen from the Afro-American Realty Company, John E. Nail and Henry C. Parker. Their response to this disenfranchisement was just as aggressive. Nail and Parker Real Estate Company bought a row of five apartment houses and evicted the white tenants. Next, they worked with other African-American groups to buy even more property. St. Philips Protestant Episcopal Church, one of the oldest and richest African-American congregations in New York, bought a row of thirteen apartment houses on 135th Street between Lenox and Seventh Avenues at a cost of $620,000 ($11,265,400 in today's dollars). The church then evicted all the white tenants and rented the apartments to blacks.

By 1910, the animosity between the two communities was beyond repair. Either the

### THE "NEGRO SCARE" RACKET

A particularly horrendous scam arose to prey on whites' fear of a black invasion. It was called the "Negro Scare" racket. The way it worked was that unscrupulous men would purchase a building in an exclusively white neighborhood and rent the apartments to blacks. The horrified white residents of the block would then attempt to buy the building to keep it segregated. The owner would initially resist selling, but would then sell the building for an outrageous price.

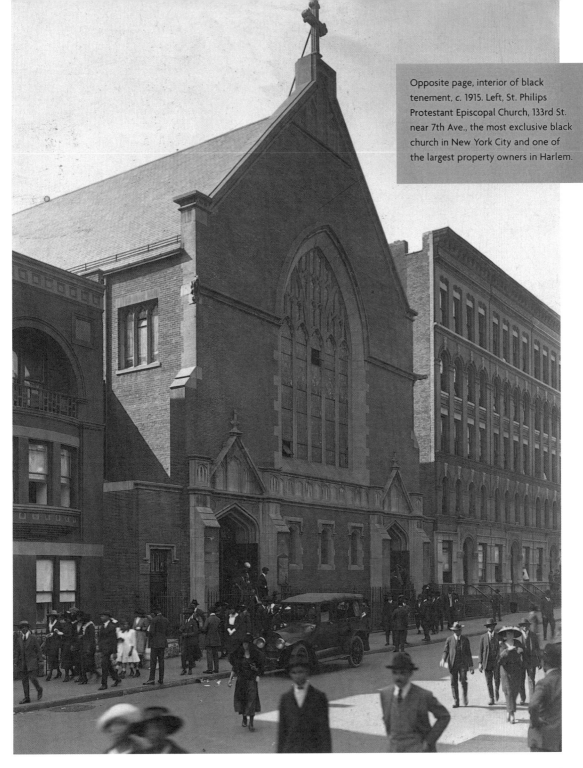

Opposite page, interior of black tenement, *c.* 1915. Left, St. Philips Protestant Episcopal Church, 133rd St. near 7th Ave., the most exclusive black church in New York City and one of the largest property owners in Harlem.

## THE LEGENDARY PIG FOOT MARY

The most legendary real estate investor in Harlem was a woman nicknamed Pig Foot Mary. She parlayed a street-corner food stand into a profitable real estate empire. Pig Foot Mary, whose real name was Lillian Harris, arrived in New York City in the fall of 1901. During her first week in New York, Mary went to work as a domestic and earned five dollars. With three of those dollars she bought a used baby carriage and a large washtub. The other two she spent on pigs' feet, a popular delicacy among Southern blacks. Then she made a deal with the owner of Rudolph's, a busy saloon near Sixty-first Street on Amsterdam Avenue, to cook the pigs' feet in his kitchen. Once prepared, she placed the entire washtub full of pigs' feet on her baby carriage and wheeled it onto the street in front of the saloon. In no time the pigs' feet were selling so fast that Mary expanded her menu and added hog-maws, chitterlings (cooked hogs' intestines), and corn-on-the-cob. To handle this wide fare, Pig Foot Mary designed and built a portable steam table, one of the first in the city, and worked her stand from early morning until late at night.

In 1917, Pig Foot Mary followed her migrant customers to Harlem, where she rented a small stall at Lenox Avenue and 135th Street. Shortly afterward, she started investing her savings in Harlem properties. Her first venture was the purchase of a Seventh Avenue apartment house for $44,000, just a few blocks from her stand. Six years later in 1923 she sold the building for $72,000. Her subsequent dealings in real estate were equally successful, and at one time her total holdings were valued at $375,000 ($3,945,000 in today's dollars).

whites or the blacks would have to go. With only the slums of Black Bohemia as an alternative, blacks doubled their efforts to move to and remain in Harlem. They not only continued to rent apartments outside the segregated zone east of Lenox Avenue but began to purchase the fine private dwellings west of Seventh Avenue as well as those bordering on St. Nicholas Park.

Whites responded to this "invasion" by abandoning the neighborhood. House after house, apartment building after apartment building, became deserted. Perhaps in a rare twist of justice, the white property owners who held out against the black tide were the ones who suffered the most in the end. While they resisted selling to blacks, their neighbors did not. Soon these white owners had nothing but empty buildings because their white tenants had moved. Eventually they were forced to sell at prices far below market value. One classic example was the Equitable Life Assurance Society sale of some eighty brick houses on West 138th Street, designed by the famous architect Stanford White. Each of these homes contained fourteen rooms, two baths, French doors, and hardwood floors. The Equitable Life Assurance Society received a mere $2,000 ($36,340 in today's dollars) for each house, at least half as much as its market value if it were located elsewhere in the city. These buildings became known as "Strivers Row," the stronghold of the black upper class.

Eventually, Harlem became such a popular destination for blacks that by the time of the Great Migration from the South to the North and a similar immigration from the West Indies, real estate prices had rocketed to incredible heights. As a result, investors who bought cheap in the depressed market made a killing. The Reverend Adam E. Clayton Powell Sr. reported the purchase of a limestone-front private house with mahogany woodwork on West 136th Street between Seventh and Eighth Avenues for $6,000 ($109,020 in today's dollars), which was resold six years later for $15,000 ($272,550 in today's dollars). By the 1920s, conservative estimates placed the total Negro ownership of Harlem property at $200 million ($1.8 billion in today's dollars).

If you ride northward the length of Manhattan Island, going through Central Park and coming out on Seventh Avenue or Lenox Avenue at One Hundred and Tenth Street, you cannot escape being struck by the sudden change in the character of the people you see. In the middle and lower parts of the city you have, perhaps, noted Negro faces here and there; but when you emerge from the Park, you see them everywhere, and as you go up either of these two great arteries leading out from the city to the north, you see more and more Negroes, walking in the streets, looking from the windows, trading in the shops, eating in the restaurants, going in and coming out of the theatres, until, nearly One Hundred and Thirty-fifth Street, ninety per cent of the people you see, including traffic officers, are Negroes.

— James Weldon Johnson, from *Black Manhattan*

Aaron Douglas illustration for the September 1927 *Crisis* cover.

# THE DAM BREAKING

## JEAN TOOMER, CLAUDE MCKAY, AND OPPORTUNITY IN THE ARTS, 1921–1924

"Up you mighty race!

You can accomplish what you will!"

— MARCUS GARVEY

## THE RISE OF A RACE

GARVEY'S FAMOUS CHANT was prophetic. African Americans everywhere began to rise as if from a deep sleep and to demand their rightful place in American culture. During the latter part of the 1920s, black pride surged. A new race-consciousness centered on self-worth emerged in nearly all walks of black life — from the rise of Harlem as a true black metropolis to the African-American heroes of World War I.

45

## 1914 SPINGARN MEDAL INSTITUTED FOR BLACK ACHIEVEMENT

Joel E. Spingarn, former chairman of the Board of Directors of the NAACP, instituted a medal to be given annually to the African-American man or woman who attained the highest achievement during the preceding year or years. Winners have been honored for their work in art, music, literature, theater, dance, photography, science, medicine, business, politics, public service, law, education, the military, civil rights, and sports. Many of the most celebrated figures of the era won this award, including the composer and baritone Harry T. Burleigh, folklorist and novelist Charles W. Chesnutt, and marine biologist Everett Just, among others.

At the beginning of the war, W. E. B. Du Bois had called upon African Americans in his famous editorial in the *Crisis* to "forget our special grievances and close our ranks shoulder to shoulder. . . . We make no ordinary sacrifice, but we make it gladly and willingly with our eyes lifted to the hills." Now they were ready to ascend that hill and receive what was rightfully theirs as citizens of a democracy.

As a result of black pride, a seismic change in American culture occurred. African Americans began to earn a long-deserved, publicly acknowledged presence on the national stage, particularly in the worlds of music, art, theater, and literature. For generations African Americans had been active in these cultural fields, but with the exception of theater their efforts had gone largely unacknowledged outside the black community. From the perspective of white culture, this emergence appeared sudden, almost instantaneous, but in reality it had been building for years. In fact, for decades much of the African-American arts had been assimilated into the national culture without any conscious acknowledgment. For example, the sacred music from black churches became popular spirituals sung by all churchgoers. Similarly, black secular music — plantation songs, ragtime, blues, jazz, and work songs — were embraced nationally. And folklore — Uncle Remus stories and other plantation tales — had been appropriated in the daily newspapers as popular bedtime stories. It took W. E. B. Du Bois and James Weldon Johnson, however, to lay the groundwork with their own novels and poetry so that writers such as Jean Toomer and Claude McKay could break the glass ceiling of artistic segregation and be celebrated for their individual achievements.

# DAM BREAKERS:
## CLAUDE MCKAY & JEAN TOOMER

UNTIL CLAUDE MCKAY published two sonnets in a 1916 issue of *Seven Arts,* a white literary publication, the last African-American poet published by whites was Paul Lawrence Dunbar just after the turn of the century. Of Dunbar's broad and varied work white publishers were interested only in his dialect poems, which were concerned with such stereotypical Negro themes as the sound of the old banjo, singing around the cabin door, and the successive seasons of watermelon, possum, and sweet potato. A classic example of the dialectal style is Dunbar's "Soliloquy of a Turkey":

> Dey's a so't o' threatenin' feelin' in de blowin' of de breeze,
> An I's feelin' kin' o' squeamish in de night;
> I's a-walkin' 'roun' a-lookin' at de diffunt style o' trees,
> An' a-measurin' dey thickness an' day height.
> Fu' dey's somep'n mighty 'spicious in de looks de da'kies give,
> Ez dey pass me an' my fambly in de groun'
> So it 'curs to me dat lakly, ef I caihs to try an' live,
> It concehns me fu' to 'mence to look erroun'. . . .

This poem is in sharp contrast to other poems by Dunbar, such as his sonnet "Harriet Beecher Stowe," an eloquent tribute to the famous abolitionist:

> She told the story, and the whole world wept
> At wrongs and cruelties it had not known
> But for this fearless woman's voice alone.
> She spoke to concsciences that long had slept:
>
> . . . . . . . . . . . . . . . . . . . . . . . . . . .
>
> Blest be the hand that dared be strong to save,
> And blest be she who in our weakness came —
> Prophet and priestess! At one stroke she gave
> A race to freedom and herself to fame.

47

"You're a lost crowd, you educated Negroes,
and you will only find your self in the roots of your own people."

The cover for Claude McKay's novel *Home to Harlem*, 1928.

At the turn of the century Dunbar in his writing had to wear the mask of the rural, uneducated Negro laborer in order to gain recognition from the wider American culture. Consequently, McKay's achievement as a poet was not just unique, it was unheard of. In keeping with the tone of the brewing racial renaissance, he removed the "Negro" mask and expressed himself in the voice of an intelligent, sensitive African American. As well, his poems expressed what the African-American masses felt, thought, and wanted to hear, and suddenly this forthright style was not to be ignored by the dominant white culture. In McKay's novel *Banjo*, the character named Ray describes what is necessary for the renaissance to succeed:

> We educated Negroes are talking a lot about a racial renaissance. And I wonder how we're going to get it. . . . If this renaissance we're talking about is going to be more than a sporadic and scabby thing, we'll have to get down to our racial roots to create it . . . [but] you're a lost crowd, you educated Negroes, and you will only find your self in the roots of your own people. You can't choose your models the haughty-minded educated white youths of a society living on its imperial conquests.

## CLAUDE McKAY, 1890–1948

Born in 1890, Festus Claude McKay grew up on a farm in Jamaica, where he was the youngest of eleven children. When he was a child, his parents steeped him in the rural farming traditions of Jamaica and passed on to him a deep sympathy for the oppressed. His early poems were written in the dialect of black country folk, with whom he felt a real kinship. As a young man, McKay came to the United States to study at Tuskegee Normal School in Alabama and later at Kansas State University, but he never completed the work necessary for a degree. Instead he moved to New York City in 1914, where he wrote for radical socialist journals such as *Seven Arts* and *Liberator*. Though McKay modeled his style on Elizabethan and Romantic lyrics, his subjects were racially militant and politically radical. He found American society hopelessly corrupted by racism and greed. His work spoke out primarily against these two evils, which won him the label of "the *enfant terrible* of the Harlem Reniassance." The candid style McKay developed focused on the depiction of an authentic blackness, and his work set the stage for the poets of the renaissance.

Claude McKay

**Two Poems by Claude McKay**

## THE WHITE HOUSE

Your door is shut against my tightened face,

And I am sharp as steel with discontent;

But I possess the courage and the grace

To bear my anger proudly and unbent.

The pavement slabs burn loose beneath my feet,

A chafing savage, down the decent street;

And passion rends my vitals as I pass,

Where boldly shines your shuttered door of glass.

Oh, I must search for wisdom every hour,

Deep in my wrathful bosom and sore and raw,

And find in it the superhuman power

To hold me to the letter of your law!

Oh, I must keep the heart inviolate

Against the potent poison of your hate.

## AMERICA

Although she feeds me bread of bitterness,

And sinks into me through her tiger's tooth,

Stealing my breath of life, I will confess

I love this cultured hell that tests my youth!

Her vigor flows like tides into my blood,

Giving me strength erect against her hate.

Her bigness sweeps my being like a flood.

Yet as a rebel fronts a king in state,

I stand within her walls with not a shred

Of terror, malice, not a word of jeer.

Darkly I gaze into the days ahead,

And see her might and granite wonders there,

Beneath the touch of Time's unerring hand.

Like priceless treasures sinking in the sand.

The open expression of authentic blackness created the feeling of racial vitality that African Americans were hungry for. The book that set the tone for this artistic explosion was Jean Toomer's brilliant novel *Cane*. Published in 1923, *Cane* was one of the first books published by the white establishment to depict African-American characters and culture authentically, rather than as caricatures. This novel and the literature it inspired rejected the old stereotypes and substituted instead notions of self-respect, self-reliance, and racial unity. William Stanley Braithwaite, the most respected black literary critic of the pre-renaissance period, wrote of Toomer's *Cane*:

> In Jean Toomer . . . we come upon the very first artist of the race, who with all an artist's passion and sympathy of life, its hurts, its sympathies, its desires, its joys, its defeats, and strange yearning, can write about the Negro without surrender or compromise of the artist's vision. . . . *Cane* is a book of gold and bronze, of dusk and flame, of ecstasy and pain, and Jean Toomer is the bright morning star of a new day of the race in literature.

Jean Toomer;
a cabin in
Sparta, Georgia,
that Toomer
photographed
in 1921.

### JEAN TOOMER, 1894–1967

Born in 1894 into the so-called black bourgeoisie, Toomer was the grandson of P. B. S. Pinchback, a light-skinned Reconstruction-era politician who made his home in Washington, D.C. Toomer was so light-skinned that he was easily mistaken for white. He was raised mostly by his grandfather, who was the first U.S. governor of African-American descent. An excellent student, he attended the University of Wisconsin to study agriculture in 1913, but he did not graduate. Instead, he sampled classes at a number of colleges and schools in Massachusetts, Chicago, and New York. By 1919, however, he had settled in New York City's Greenwich Village and set out to become a writer. By 1921, he became restless and accepted a position as a substitute teacher at a black school in a part of rural Georgia. His two months in Sparta, Georgia, introduced him to the abject poverty of black rural life as well as its rich musical and folk traditions. There, he witnessed for the first time the barely submerged fears and frustrations of black people who were facing discrimination and violence in the South. On his return trip north, Toomer began to form his initial ideas for the book that would become *Cane*. Although called a novel, *Cane* is a mixture of poetry, fiction, and drama that defies classification but is often called "experimental fiction." The work is essentially fragments that come together, much like a patchwork quilt, to create a unified narrative. Most important, Toomer's *Cane* created a standard of excellence for the literature of the Harlem Renaissance.

**Excerpt from Toomer's** *Cane*

## KABNIS

Ralph Kabnis, propped in his bed, tried to read. To read himself to sleep. An oil lamp on a chair near his elbow burns unsteadily. The cabin room is spaced fantastically about it. Whitewashed hearth and chimney, black with sooty sawteeth. Ceiling, patterned by the fringed globe of the lamp. The walls, unpainted, are seasoned a rosin yellow. And cracks between the boards are black. These cracks are the lips the night winds use for whispering. Night winds in Georgia are vagrant poets, whispering. Kabnis, against his will, lets his books slip down, and listens to them. The warm whiteness of his bed, the lamp-light, do not protect him from the weird chill of their song:

> White-man's land.
> Niggers, sing.
> Burn, bear black children
> Till poor rivers bring
> Rest, and sweet glory
> In Camp Ground.

Kabnis' thin hair is streaked on the pillow. His hand strokes the slim silk of his mustache. His thumb, pressed under his chin, seems to be trying to give squareness and projection to it. Brown eyes stare from a lemon face. Moisture gathers beneath his arm-pits. He slides down beneath the cover, seeking release.

Kabnis: Near me. Now. Whoever you are, my warm glowing sweetheart, do not think that the face that rests beside you is the real Kabnis. Ralph Kabnis is a dream. And dreams are faces with large eyes and weak chins and broad brows that get smashed by the fists of square faces. The body of the world is bull-necked. A dream is a soft face that fits uncertainly upon it . . . God, if I could develop that in words. Give what I know a bull-neck and a heaving body, all would go well with me, wouldn't it, sweetheart? If I could feel that I came to the South to face it. If I, the dream (not what is weak and afraid in me) could become the face of the South. How my lips would sing for it, my songs being the lips of its soul. Soul. Soul hell. There aint no such thing. What in hell was that?

## THE FLOWERING OF THE RENAISSANCE

ETWEEN THE END of World War I and 1924, serious works by African Americans were published and laid the foundation for more to come. W. E. B. Du Bois published *Darkwater,* a collection of essays, in 1920, and in 1921 Benjamin Brawley's groundbreaking *A Social History of the American Negro* appeared in print. But the renaissance truly began with the publication of a book of poems, *Harlem Shadows,* by Claude McKay in 1922. This collection contains his most famous sonnets, "If We Must Die," "The White House," "America," and "The Lynching." That same year poet Georgia Douglass Johnson's *Bronze* and James Weldon Johnson's *Book of American Negro Poetry* appeared. James Weldon Johnson explained the importance of these works in the introduction to his *Book of American Negro Poetry:*

No people that has produced great literature and art has ever been looked upon by the world as distinctly inferior.... The status of the Negro in the United States is more a question of national mental attitude toward the race than of actual conditions. And nothing will do more to change that mental attitude and raise his status than a demonstration of intellectual parity by the Negro through the production of literature and art.

Johnson's bold assertions characterized the sentiment among African-American writers in the early twenties. Their impulse was toward either a "raceless" literature that demonstrated just how little blacks differed from whites, or a literature of "uplift" that would raise African Americans' intellectual status to a level of parity with whites. The most notable of this group was Du Bois's protégé Jessie Redmond Fauset. Her novel *There Is Confusion* explored how blacks in large cities, such as New York, could find their identity amid the myths and social constructs of the dominant white culture. Black critic George S. Schuyler took Johnson's argument about "intellectual parity" even further. Schuyler made a famous defense of "universal" literature in his essay "The Negro-Art Hokum," in which he argued that blacks and whites live in the same culture, not in two separate ones, and thus their literature should not be different from one another.

Details from "Drawing for Mulattoes – Number 4" by Richard Bruce in *Ebony and Topaz.*

[W]hen he responds to the same political, social, moral, and economic stimuli in precisely the same manner as his white neighbor, it is sheer nonsense to talk about "racial differences" as between the American black man and the American white man. Glance over a Negro newspaper (it is printed in good Americanese) and you will find the usual quota of crime news, scandal, personals, and uplift to be found in the average white newspaper — which, by the way, is more widely read by the Negroes than is the Negro press. In order to satisfy the cravings of an inferiority complex engendered by the colorphobia of the mob, the readers of the Negro newspapers are given a slight dash of racialistic seasoning. In the homes of black and white Americans of the same cultural and economic level one finds similar furniture, literature, and conversation. How, then, can the black American be expected to produce art and literature dissimilar to that of the white American?

Schuyler and others were correct in asserting that African Americans are no different than whites, but they were mistaken in deeming similar the intellectual, emotional, and spiritual — in short, universal — experiences of all Americans in the same socioeconomic class. Without question, the black experience in a white culture is profoundly different than the white experience. Blacks simply did not have the same freedom and opportunity. Consequently, what made writers such as Jean Toomer and Claude McKay so powerful was their ability to express an authentic black experience that was simultaneously rooted in the particulars of black life and involved in themes universal to all humankind. The notion of a "raceless" literature is limited to universal themes that affect all people, thus it cannot address cultural minutiae of a particular community.

**"In the homes of black and white Americans of the same cultural and economic level one finds similar furniture, literature, and conversation. How, then, can the black American be expected to produce art and literature dissimilar to that of the white American?"**

Detail of Aaron Douglas cover illustration for *FIRE!!*

# FIRE!!

## AN EXPLOSION OF CREATIVITY

> FIRE . . . a cry of conquest in the night warning
> those who sleep and revitalizing those who
> linger in the quiet places dozing. . . .
> "Fy-ah,
> Fy-ah, Lawd,
> Fy-ah gonna burn ma soul!"
>
> — Foreword to the literary magazine *FIRE!!*

## THE MATCH

STRIKE A MATCH and the white-hot flame will crackle and pop. The intense light will blind and dazzle. The fierce heat will burn and singe. Its spark will give energy where only dormant matter existed before. In 1923, Harlem was a match ready to be ignited. All that was needed was the right person, at the right time, to strike it. That person had to be someone who would not simply light the match but also feed the fire. Harlem was now crowded with explosive talent and creativity, but the fuse hadn't been lit. That is, until Charles Spurgeon Johnson moved to Harlem from Chicago.

## CHARLES SPURGEON JOHNSON
### 1893–1956

Born in 1893 in Bristol, Virginia, Charles Spurgeon Johnson was the son of a Baptist minister and grew up in a secure middle-class family. Later in life he described his father as an atypical black minister because of the elder Johnson's "quality and security of his education." From an early age Johnson was required to study the classics of Western literature, theology, and history. Before he left home at fourteen to attend Wayland Academy in Richmond, Virginia, he had been reading — "though not necessarily always absorbing" — such works as the *Lives of the Saints*, the sermons of Spurgeon, Greek mythology, Gibbons's *Rise and Fall of the Roman Empire*, and countless dimestore mysteries and adventure novels. In 1916 Johnson graduated from Virginia Union University, finishing in three years. From there he moved to the University of Chicago, where he did graduate work in sociology. His studies were interrupted by World War I, where he saw action as a regimental sergeant major in the 103rd Pioneer Infantry. After the war he was a major contributor to the 1922 book *The Negro in Chicago: A Study of Race Relations and a Race Riot*. From there, he went to New York to work for the National Urban League, where he directed economic and sociological research. At this time he also edited the National Urban League's magazine, *Opportunity: A Journal of Negro Life*, which became one of the era's biggest supporters of African-American literature and arts. After organizing the famous Civic Club Dinner, Johnson edited an anthology of renaissance prose and poetry titled *Ebony and Topaz*, published in 1927. By the next year Johnson felt that the momentum of the renaissance was assured, so he left New York for Nashville and Fisk University's sociology department. Johnson eventually became Fisk's first African-American president, and over the next few decades he became one of America's most respected and honored sociologists.

Johnson wasn't an artist himself. He was a sociologist who had made a name for himself in Chicago for his groundbreaking work on racism. In 1923 he left a promising career as a scholar to come to Harlem not simply to study but to put into practice his ideas about combating racism — ideas that were considered radical at the time. From his earlier studies Johnson had become convinced that blacks and whites would someday live in equality. He believed that blacks and whites would finally "cut across and eventually undermine all barriers of racial segregation and caste." He had the visionary idea that whites would accept and appreciate blacks simply by hanging out with them in the same places — sharing ideas, meals, and work. Johnson dedicated himself tirelessly to this mission by promoting and publishing black artists during the renaissance and afterward.

According to Langston Hughes, Johnson "did more to encourage and develop Negro writers during the 1920s than anyone else in America." As founder and editor of the National Urban League's *Opportunity: A Journal of Negro Life,* Johnson was determined to help African-American writers and artists gain recognition beyond the boundaries of Harlem and the small black communities scattered across America. The initial mission of *Opportunity* was to "depict Negro life as it is with no exaggerations. We shall try to set down interestingly but without sugar-coating or generalization the findings of careful scientific surveys and the facts gathered from research." Johnson expanded that purpose in the next issue to reach beyond cold, hard facts and figures to include "the cultural side of Negro life that has been long neglected." He knew that people would need to see the souls of African Americans in order to understand them, and that that could only be done through the arts. His mission for the journal, and himself, was to make public the exciting poems, stories, essays, photographs, and artwork of African Americans who explored authentic black cultural life.

Johnson found that publishing the work of African Americans in *Opportunity* and waiting for readers to discover them was too slow a process. He wanted results right away, and with good reason. Johnson knew that an author's publication in *Opportunity* would never guarantee mainstream literary success, much less break down the barriers of the white publishing world. He'd also been observing the writers he published struggle

**He knew that people would need to see the souls of African Americans in order to understand them, and that that could only be done through the arts.**

"What American literature needs at this moment is color,

If the Negroes are not in a position to contribute these items,

Jessie Fauset

OPPORTUNITY
A JOURNAL OF NEGRO LIFE

MAY, 1927

15¢

to get by with low-paying jobs as busboys, bell-hops, porters, and maids. In fact, the most famous writer of the renaissance, Langston Hughes, made his living as a busboy while his poems appeared in such acclaimed publications as *Harper's* magazine, *Opportunity,* and the *Crisis.* Novelist Wallace Thurman and poet Arna Bontemps worked for the Los Angeles post office. Artist Aaron Douglas was a poorly paid teacher in a segregated Kansas City school. Johnson knew that there were many other talented African Americans who had to sacrifice their gifts to make the rent and put food on the table. He worried that it would be just a matter of time before their spirits would be broken just like the generation before and the generation before that.

With the weight of the Urban League and *Opportunity* behind him, Johnson fought this tragedy-in-the-making every way he could. He started contests with substantial prizes of $100 or more. At the time this was a considerable amount of money, when most blacks made much less than that in a month. These prizes brought publicity to the Harlem writers, but more was needed to establish them as important authors in the minds — and pocketbooks — of the larger, more powerful white community. A "coming-out party" was Johnson's answer. He calculated that if he could get influential editors and publishers in the same room with Harlem's literati, he could persuade them to recognize the immense talent in the black community. With that recognition, black writers and artists could gain the widespread publication and financial support they deserved. At the beginning of 1924 Johnson began planning a literary extravaganza,

music, gusto, the free expression of gay or desperate moods.
I do not know what Americans are."

— Carl Van Doren, editor of *Century Magazine*, at the Civic Club Dinner

the likes of which had never been seen in New York before. He initially used the publication of Jessie Redmond Fauset's first novel, *There Is Confusion,* as the reason for the event. Fauset was the literary editor of the *Crisis* and one of the most respected writers among the more established artists.

The event, however, quickly evolved beyond one author's book party and into a full-scale celebration of African-American literature called the Civic Club Dinner. Johnson enlisted the help of white railroad heir and Urban League board member William H. Baldwin III, who took to the task with enthusiasm. Baldwin appealed to numerous movers and shakers of the downtown publishing world, especially Frederick Lewis Allen, the Harper & Brothers editor. Baldwin later wrote, "Allen invited a 'small but representative group from his field,' and Charles S. Johnson 'supplied an equally representative group of Negroes.'"

Portrait of Countee Cullen by Winold Reiss.

## THE TINDERBOX

A group of the younger writers, which includes Eric Walrond, Jessie Fauset, Gwendolyn Bennett, Countee Cullen, Langston Hughes, Alain Locke, and some others [would be at the Civic Club]. . . . I think you might find this group interesting at least enough to draw you away for a few hours from your work on your next book.

S O READ CHARLES S. Johnson's invitation to Jean Toomer. The dinner was planned for March 21, 1924, at New York's only integrated upper-crust club, the Civic Club, on Twelfth Street near Fifth Avenue, and all the Harlem literati were invited.

**A report of the celebrated dinner appeared shortly after in *Opportunity***

## THE DEBUT OF THE YOUNGER SCHOOL OF NEGRO WRITERS

Interest among the literati of New York in the emerging group of younger Negro writers found an expression in a recent meeting of the Writers' Guild, an informal group whose membership includes Countee Cullen, Eric Walrond, Langston Hughes, Jessie Fauset, Gwendolyn Bennett, Harold Jackman, Regina Anderson, and a few others. The occasion was a "coming out party," at the Civic Club, on March 21 — a date selected around the appearance of the novel "There Is Confusion" by Jessie Fauset. The responses to the invitations sent out were immediate and enthusiastic and the few regrets that came in were genuine.

Although there was no formal, prearranged program, the occasion provoked a surprising spontaneity of expression from both the members of the writers' group and from the distinguished visitors present.

A brief interpretation of the object of the Guild was given by Charles S. Johnson, Editor of *Opportunity,* who introduced Alain Locke, virtual don of the movement, who had been selected to act as Master of Ceremonies and to interpret the new currents manifest in the literature of this younger school. Alain Locke has been one of the most resolute stimulators of this group, and although he has been writing longer than most of them, he is distinctly a part of the movement. One excerpt reflects the tenor of his remarks. He said: "They sense within their group — meaning the Negro group — a spiritual wealth which if they can properly expound will be ample for a new judgment and re-appraisal of the race."

Horace Liveright, publisher, told about the difficulties, even yet, of marketing books of admitted merit. The value of a book cannot be gauged by the sales. He regarded Jean Toomer's "Cane" as one of the most interesting that he had handled and yet, less than 500 copies had been sold. In his exhortations to the younger group he warned against the danger of reflecting in one's own writings the "inferiority complex" which is so insistently and frequently apparent in an overbalanced emphasis on "impossibly good" fiction types. He felt that to do the best writing it was necessary to give a rounded picture which included bad types as well as good ones since both of these go to make up life.

Dr. W. E. B. Du Bois made his first public appearance and address since his return to this country from Africa. He was introduced by the chairman with soft seriousness as a representative of the "older school." Dr. Du Bois explained that the Negro writers of a few years back were of necessity pioneers, and much of their style was forced upon them by the barriers against publication of literature about Negroes of any sort.

James Weldon Johnson was introduced as an anthologist of Negro verse and one who had given invaluable encouragement to the work of this younger group.

Carl Van Doren, Editor of the *Century,* spoke on the future of imaginative writing among Negroes. His remarks are given in full elsewhere in this issue.

Another young Negro writer, Walter F. White, whose novel "Fire in Flint" has been accepted for publication, also spoke and made reference to the passing of the stereotypes of the Negroes of fiction.

Professor Montgomery Gregory of Howard University, who came from Washington for the meeting, talked about the possibilities of Negroes in drama and told of the work of several talented Negro writers in this field, some of whose plays were just coming into recognition.

Another visitor from Philidelphia, Dr. Albert C. Barnes, art connoisseur and foremost authority in America on primitive Negro art, sketched the growing interest in this art which had had such tremendous influence on the entire modern art movement.

Miss Jessie Fauset was given a place of distinction on the program. She paid her respects to those friends who had contributed to her accomplishment, acknowledging a particular debt to her "best friend and severest critic" Dr. Du Bois.

The original poems read by Countee Cullen were received with tremendous ovation. Miss Gwendolyn Bennett's poem, dedicated to the occasion, is reproduced. It is called

"To Usward"
Let us be still
As ginger jars are still
Upon a Chinese shelf,
And let us be contained
By entities of Self. . . .

Not still with lethargy and sloth,
But quiet with the pushing of our growth;
Not self-contained with smug identity,
But conscious of the strength in entity.

## THE NEW NEGRO

### EDITED BY ALAIN LOCKE

▼▼▼▼▼CONTENTS▼▼▼▼▼

## THE FIRE!

THE BLAZING ENERGY that emerged from the Civic Club Dinner set the Harlem literary scene on fire. Younger writers — such as Langston Hughes, Wallace Thurman, Nella Larson, and Zora Neale Hurston — left the event feeling that they would now find the interest and support to pursue their work, while older artists had their efforts affirmed by the powerful editors and publishers of the New York book and magazine world. This excitement translated into a number of new publications that celebrated the men and women of the Harlem Renaissance.

Paul Kellogg, the white editor of the white publication *Survey Graphic,* lingered after the dinner to talk with Countee Cullen, Jessie Fauset, and others. Out of this conversation came the idea for a special black cultural issue of *Survey Graphic,* which billed itself as a monthly magazine for professionals who "want to know of the living contributions of other professions where they overlap yours in the realm of common welfare." Kellogg quickly offered Charles S. Johnson control of the March 1925 issue, which would be devoted entirely to black culture. Johnson wrote Ethel Ray Nance, a woman whom he wanted to move to New York to be his secretary, "A big plug was bitten off. Now it's a question of living up to the reputation. Yes, I should have added, a stream of manuscripts has started into my office . . ."

Johnson quickly enlisted critic and essayist Alain Locke as the editor of this special issue, which was titled *Harlem: Mecca of the New Negro.* Nearly every writer of importance to the Harlem Renaissance was included.

Johnson didn't stop with the publication of one anthology. He went on to edit another one, *Ebony and Topaz.* As well, he badgered writers and artists all over the country to move to New York so that Harlem would truly be the "Mecca of the New Negro." He convinced both poet Arna Bontemps and novelist Wallace Thurman to leave their jobs at the Los Angeles post office. He encouraged novelist and folklore anthologist Zora Neale Hurston, then a sophomore at Howard University, to come. The artist Aaron Douglas was on the fast track to becoming a principal at a segregated high school in Kansas City when Johnson got word of Douglas's talent. Harlem was plentiful with writers, but there were few visual artists. Johnson instructed his secretary, Ethel Ray Nance, to insist on Douglas's moving to Harlem. "Better to be a dishwasher in New York than to be head of a high school in Kansas City," she cajoled after several of her more polite entreaties were ignored. How could Douglas resist? Harlem was the center of the world for the African-American arts. If he had any ambition to be a working artist, he would have to come to Harlem. Consequently, he did and he worked on the *Survey Graphic* issue with German artist Winold Reiss.

Next, Charles S. Johnson established the *Opportunity* literary awards to help the arriving artists and writers establish themselves. On the editorial page of the August 1924 issue, he announced the new prizes to be awarded:

---

## OPPORTUNITY LITERARY CONTEST

To stimulate creative expression among Negroes and to direct attention to the rich and unexploited sources of materials for literature in Negro life, Opportunity will offer prizes for short stories, poetry, plays, essays, and personal experience sketches to the amount of

### FIVE HUNDRED DOLLARS

There will be three awards for each division. . . . If you can write, this is your Opportunity.

---

Johnson enlisted nineteen respected white and black editors, publishers, and artists to judge the contest. These included Robert C. Benchley, novelist, drama critic, and editor of *Life* magazine; Alexander Woolcott, drama critic for the New York *Sun*; Dorothy Canfield Fisher, novelist; Carl Van Doren, editor of *Century Magazine*; and Montgomery Gregory, director of the Department

Miguel Covarrubias's illustration for Hughes's first book *The Weary Blues*.

## THE WEARY BLUES

Droning a drowsy syncopated tune,
Rocking back and forth to a mellow croon,
    I heard a Negro play.
Down on Lenox Avenue the other night
By the pale dull pallor of an old gas light
    He did a lazy sway . . .
    He did a lazy sway . . .
To the tune o' those Weary Blues.
With his ebony hands on each ivory key
He made that poor piano moan with melody.
    O Blues!
Swaying to and fro on his rickety stool
He played that sad raggy tune like a musical fool.
    Sweet Blues!

Coming from a black man's soul.
    O Blues!
In a deep song voice with a melancholy tone
I heard that Negro sing, that old piano moan —
    "Ain't got nobody in all this world,
    Ain't got nobody but ma self.
    I's gwine to quit ma frownin'
    And put ma troubles on the shelf."
Thump, thump, thump, went his foot on the floor.
He played a few chords then sang some more —
    "I got the Weary Blues
    And I can't be satisfied.
    Got the Weary Blues
    And can't be satisfied —
    I ain't happy no mo'
    And I wish that I had died."
And far into the night he crooned that tune.
The stars went out and so did the moon.
The singer stopped playing and went to bed
While the Weary Blues echoed through his head.
He slept like a rock or a man that's dead.
                    —LANGSTON HUGHES

"In some places the autumn of 1924 may have been an unremarkable season. In Harlem, it was like a foretaste of paradise. A blue haze descended at night and with it strings of fairy lights on the broad avenues."

— Poet Arna Bontemps

of Dramatics at Howard University, among others. The prize money was donated by Mrs. Henry G. Leach, wife of the editor of *Forum,* a mainstream white journal. In May of 1925, the winners were anounced: Langston Hughes's poem "The Weary Blues" won first prize for poetry, and it would become the poetic emblem of the renaissance.

Charles S. Johnson was not the sole promoter of the Harlem Renaissance. The NAACP journal, the *Crisis,* also began offering writing awards. The March 1925 *Survey Graphic* issue was published into an expanded anthology, *The New Negro,* which became the standard volume of the era. Many of the writers and artists now found themselves being published in the white mainstream publications. Poets Georgia Douglass Johnson, Frank Horne, Arna Bontemps, Langston Hughes, and Countee Cullen saw their work appear in numerous magazines, such as *Harper's* and *Century,* and had their books published by mainstream publishers. Championed by bestselling white novelist Fannie Hurst, anthropologist and writer Zora Neale Hurston published several stories, plays, and collections of folklore. Walter White, a powerful member of the NAACP, wrote two novels about the horrors of the South, and also wrote *Rope* and *Faggot,* two incendiary histories about the lynching and burning of black people in America. Jessie Fauset, an editor at the *Crisis,* wrote novels, including *There Is Confusion,* while Claude McKay wrote the novel *Banjo.* All of this work and more was making its way into print and being distributed among white literary circles, where previously none would have had a chance at publication.

"What Mr. Van Vechten has written is just what those

## THE RIFT

SIMMERING BELOW THE surface of the renaissance's blazing creativity was a rift that went unacknowledged until one of the most controversial novels of the age appeared on the scene — *Nigger Heaven*. Written by Carl Van Vechten, a white critic and Harlem enthusiast, *Nigger Heaven* was published in 1926 and quickly became a bestseller. Largely forgotten today, the novel wallowed in what Van Vechten believed to be the "squalor of Negro life, the vice of Negro life." Its plot was overwrought and melodramatic in its portrayal of a young man who deserts his true love for the exotic mysteries of an older woman. When this woman rejects him for another man, the young man attempts to murder his usurper. *Nigger Heaven* was the first fictional treatment of Harlem and African-American urban life written by a white. As a novelty, it created a storm in the general media, but many Harlemites felt betrayed by Van Vechten, to whom they had opened their doors. Richetta Randolph, James Weldon Johnson's secretary, summed up her shock in a letter to a vacationing Johnson: "To the very end I hoped for something which would make me feel that he had done Negro Harlem a service with his work. . . . What Mr. Van Vechten has written is just what those who do not know us think about all of us."

Members of the Talented Tenth uniformly boycotted the book. Du Bois called it "a blow in the face" and "an affront to the hospitality of black folk and the intelligence of white." Not simply offended by the use of "nigger" in its title, many black intellectuals were fearful that the portrayal of African Americans in what they perceived as the crudest of stereotypes would only continue to support racial biases. Their response underscored their convictions about the role of literature in African-American life — namely, that literature by and about blacks should serve primarily as propaganda. This meant that works of artistic merit should be untainted by stereotypes and embarrassing vulgarities. They believed that too much blackness, too much street culture, and too much folklore would undermine blacks' ability to gain respect and equality in the dominant white culture. For them, art was meant to teach the white world about blacks and to convince them of the enduring value of African-American culture. Their horror at the publication of *Nigger Heaven,* then, was no surprise.

Above, Carl Van Vechten. Right, a caricature of Van Vechten by Miguel Covarrubias as an African American.

who do not know us think about all of us."

— Richetta Randolph, James Weldon Johnson's secretary

The true shock, however, was that not all blacks agreed with the Talented Tenth. Many of the younger generation of black writers and artists — Wallace Thurman and Langston Hughes, among others — praised Van Vechten's novel, although some bemoaned the use of "nigger" in the title. These young mavericks saw the success of *Nigger Heaven* as permission for them to celebrate blackness in all its manifestations, not just the portrayals approved by Talented Tenth society. This newfound freedom was so welcome that in response to the majority's withering attacks on Van Vechten, Wallace Thurman and others suggested erecting a monument to the author. What the young writers most

**"Nigger Heaven! That's what Harlem is. We sit in our places in the gallery of New York theatre and watch the white world sitting down below in the good seats in the orchestra. . . . It never seems to occur to them that Nigger Heaven is crowded, that there isn't another seat, that something has to be done."**

— Carl Van Vechten, from *Nigger Heaven*

admired about the novel was its use of African-American slang to convey not just local color but what they believed were serious ideas. Because of this, they resisted the literary limits set by their elders. They knew the Talented Tenth represented only a small fraction of the larger black community, whereas the young writers sought to speak for the entire population of Harlem. For them, to ignore the larger Harlem was to do it injustice. Thus, works like Hughes's "The Weary Blues" explored a wider range of experience. Although that poem won an award, much of the work about greater Harlem went unpublished and unread.

That is, until novelist and critic Wallace Thurman decided to create his own journal in 1926. He named the journal *FIRE!!* With two exclamation points in the title, there was no mistaking Thurman and his fellow editors' stalwart intentions. In addition to staking out their own artistic principles, they wanted to confront the establishment aggressively.

*FIRE!!* expressed and celebrated those aspects of Harlem that the Talented Tenth were afraid of: sex; color-consciousness; racism; self-hatred among blacks; and the perception of blacks as "primitive," "decadent," wild, colorful, and dangerous "Negroes." One of the first and most vocal writers to join in Thurman's call to arms was Zora Neale Hurston. She was fearless in recording the rural folktales and sermons that embarrassed the Talented Tenth, and she portrayed low-class blacks in her fiction. The following passage comes from Hurston's story "Sweat," which first appeared in *FIRE!!* It is one of the first pieces Hurston published and it examines the lives of black laborers in authentic circumstances.

**"Vivid, hot designs upon an ebony bordered loom . . . satisfy pagan thirst for beauty unadorned."**

It was eleven o'clock of a Spring night in Florida. It was Sunday. Any other night, Delia Jones would have been in bed for two hours by this time. But she was a washwoman, and Monday morning meant a great deal to her. So she collected the soiled clothes on Saturday when she returned the clean things. Sunday night after church, she sorted them and put the white things to soak. It saved her almost a half day's start. A great hamper in the bedroom held the clothes that she brought home. It was so much neater than a number of bundles lying around.

She squatted in the kitchen floor beside the great pile of clothes, sorting them into small heaps according to color, and humming a song in a mournful key, but wondering through it all where Sykes, her husband, had gone with her horse and buckboard.

Just then something long, round, limp and black fell upon her shoulders and slithered to the floor beside her. A great terror took hold of her. It softened her knees and dried her mouth so that it was a full minute before she could cry out or move. Then she saw that it was the big bull whip her husband liked to carry when he drove.

She lifted her eyes to the door and saw him standing there bent over with laughter at her fright. She screamed at him.

"Sykes, what you throw dat whip on me like dat? You know it would skeer me — looks just like a snake, an' you knows how skeered Ah is of snakes."

**Two Poems from *FIRE!! A Quarterly Devoted to Younger Negro Artists***

## LITTLE CINDERELLA

Look me over, kid!
I knows I'm neat —
Little Cinderella from head to feet.
Drinks all night at Club Alabam, —
What comes next I don't give a damn!

Daddy, daddy,
You sho' looks keen!
I likes men that are long and lean.
Broad street ain't got no brighter lights
Than your eyes at pitch midnight.

— LEWIS ALEXANDER

## JUNGLE TASTE

There is a coarseness
In the songs of black men
Coarse as the songs
Of the sea.
There is a weird strangeness
In the songs of black men
Which sounds not strange
To me.

There is beauty
In the faces of black women,
Jungle beauty
And mystery.
Dark, hidden beauty
In the faces of black women
Which only black men
See.

— EDWARD SILVERA

A year later Langston Hughes boldly articulated this new literature's aim to portray "authentic" views of black life:

> [I]t is the duty of the younger Negro artist ... to change through the force of his art that old whispering "I want to be white," hidden in the aspiration of his people, to "Why should I want to be white? I am a Negro — and beautiful!" ... We younger Negro artists who create now intend to express our individual dark-skinned selves without fear or shame.... We know we are beautiful. And ugly too. The tom-tom cries and the tom-tom laughs.... We build our temples for tomorrow, strong as we know how, and we stand on top of the mountain, free within ourselves.

In this article, which appeared in the *Nation* magazine, Hughes voiced the sentiment that a generation later would become a rallying cry for black consciousness: "Black is beautiful." The blossoming of that pride added fuel to the fire that crackled in Harlem after the renaissance had officially begun.

## THREE FIGURES TO EMERGE OUT OF THE FIRE

### WALLACE THURMAN

ALTHOUGH HE DIED young, Wallace Thurman was not simply a cheerleader for black writers but a vocal critic and theorist who promoted controversial themes. Thurman was born August 16, 1902, in Salt Lake City. His father, Oscar Thurman, played no role in his childhood, having abandoned the family for California. Though his mother, Beulah, was present, the most important person for him was his maternal grandmother, Emma "Ma Jack" Jackson, to whom he dedicated his first novel, *The Blacker the Berry*. Thurman grew up nervous and sickly but very devoted to books and movies. His reading ranged far and wide, including Dostoyevsky, Freud, Nietzsche, and Shakespeare. He attended the University of Utah and then the University of Southern California, but he did not complete a degree. By 1923 he was working in the Los Angeles post office but was driven by greater literary ambitions. He tried to publish a short-lived literary magazine and organized a literary group comparable to what was happening in Harlem. In August of 1925, however, he abandoned Los Angeles for Harlem, where he quickly established himself as a rising star. He worked at a number of African-American newspapers and ended up as managing editor of *The Messenger*. Thurman and Langston Hughes roomed together and collaborated on the literary magazine *FIRE!!* The foreword declared that this publication intended to weave "vivid, hot designs upon an ebony bordered loom and . . . satisfy pagan thirst for beauty unadorned." At the time, the magazine was ignored by critics, but later *FIRE!!* became recognized as one of the most influential publications of the period in terms of artistic merit. Nevertheless, it was a financial disaster, and when the building that stored the copies of the magazine burned down, *FIRE!!* literally went up in smoke. Thurman's own salary was ultimately tapped to pay the $1000 debt ($10,340 in today's dollars).

Undaunted by failure, Thurman decided to launch a new project as editor of *Harlem: A Forum of Negro Life. Harlem* was published in November of 1928. This magazine was meant to be different from *FIRE!!*, in that it would contain both racial and nonracial subject matter. It suffered, however, the same fate as did *FIRE!!* and went under. At this point a discouraged Thurman turned to playwriting, and with William Jourdan Rapp he wrote *Harlem,* which was based on Thurman's short story in *FIRE!!* The play brought the rent party and the Harlem numbers racket to Broadway and was a critical and financial success downtown. In 1929 Thurman's first novel, *The Blacker the Berry,* was published. The novel is about a young woman's struggle with racism both in the black community and beyond. His next novel, *Infants of the Spring,* appeared in 1932 and is a scathing indictment of the Harlem Renaissance. By this time, however, Thurman's drinking and depression were growing worse and worse. His last

novel, *The Interne,* was a collaboration with A. L. Furman and was a sort of exposé of the medical profession. The book was panned by critics. Around this time he moved to Hollywood to write screenplays. His script *Tomorrow's Children* was produced in 1934. In May of 1934, he returned to Harlem and collapsed at a party shortly thereafter. On December 21 he died of tuberculosis at age 32. His screenplay *High School Girls* was produced in 1935. Both of his films were ignored. Thurman's legacy was his fearlessness in the face of opposition and indifference by both blacks and whites. He was one of the pioneers of unflinchingly authentic themes that led the way for the next generation of writers.

**Wallace Thurman, 1902–1934**

## LANGSTON HUGHES

THE MOST IMPORTANT poet to emerge from the renaissance, Langston Hughes was also a member of one of black America's most respected families. His maternal grandfather was one of the band of men who joined John Brown in his raid on Harper's Ferry in 1859. The raid was a desperate attempt to ignite an insurgency that would free Southern slaves. Hughes's grandmother wore his grandfather's bullet-ridden shawl every day of her remaining life. Amid this legacy James Mercer Langston Hughes was born in Joplin, Missouri, on February 1, 1902. His mother, Carrie Langston Hughes, had been a schoolteacher; his father, James Nathaniel Hughes, was a lawyer and moved to Mexico out of frustration while his son was still an infant. Langston Hughes was raised primarily by his grandmother, Mary Langston. As a teen Hughes moved in with his mother in Illinois after she remarried. Upon graduation from an integrated high school in Cleveland, he moved to Mexico with his father and spent a year teaching there. In 1921 he returned to the United States, and a few months after his poem "The Negro Speaks of Rivers" appeared in the June 1921 issue of the *Crisis,* Hughes began attending Columbia University. After a year in school Hughes left to work in New York, on transatlantic ships, and in Paris until 1925.

While working as a busboy in Washington, D.C., Hughes slipped three poems beside poet and editor Vachel Lindsay's plate. Lindsay was impressed enough to promote Hughes to influential editors. In 1925 Hughes won the *Opportunity* literary contest, and his first collection of poems, *The Weary Blues,* appeared in 1926. Hughes was one of the few black writers who was able to support himself financially by writing, but not until well into middle age. He published poems, stories, screenplays, articles, children's books, and songs during his lifetime. He spent much of his life promoting black writers by compiling anthologies of African-American poetry. He received the NAACP's Spingarn Medal in 1960 and was elected to the National Institute of Arts and Letters in 1961. He died of congestive heart failure in New York City on May 22, 1967, at the age of 65.

Langston Hughes
1902–1967

## ZORA NEALE HURSTON

ONE OF THE first to collect African-American folklore, Hurston was both an acclaimed anthropologist and novelist. According to the genealogy recorded in the Hurston family Bible, Zora Neale Hurston was born January 15, 1891, in Notasulga, Alabama. She was raised in America's first all-black incorporated town, Eatonville, Florida. Her father, John Hurston, was a carpenter, preacher, and three-term mayor in Eatonville. Her mother, Lucy Hurston, died in 1904, after which Zora was sent away to school. In 1917 she began studies at Morgan Academy in Baltimore and in 1918 attended Howard University, where her first short story appeared in the college literary magazine. She later won a scholarship to Barnard College to study with the eminent anthropologist Franz Boas.

In New York, Hurston was secretary to a bestselling novelist of the time, Fannie Hurst, and was a major force in the Harlem Renaissance. She was associate publisher of the avant-garde journal *FIRE!!* and collaborated with a number of writers on several plays, including *Mule Bone: A Comedy of Negro Life,* written with Langston Hughes. Hurston traveled through the South, as well as Latin American countries and Jamaica, to collect folklore. The tales were collected into two books, *Mules and Men* (1935) and *Tell My Horse* (1938). Her first novel, *Jonah's Gourd Vine,* appeared in 1934 and is based on the lives of her parents in Eatonville. Her most acclaimed novel, *Their Eyes*

Zora Neale Hurston,
1891–1960

*Were Watching God,* was published in 1937 and was written after a failed love affair. The novel explores a middle-aged woman's journey toward self-realization in a sexist society. Her autobiography, *Dust Tracks on a Road,* won the 1943 Annisfield Award. Her last novel, *Seraph on the Suwanee,* was her only work to include white protagonists. During her later years she worked as a maid and wrote for a number of magazines, but her increasing conservatism isolated her from her peers. She died on January 28, 1960, in Fort Pierce, Florida.

*Harlem at Night*, Winold Reiss.

# A SOCIAL BREAKTHROUGH

We have tomorrow
Bright before us
Like a flame

Yesterday, a night-gone thing
A sun-down name.

And Dawn today
Broad arch above the road we came.

We march!

— LANGSTON HUGHES

## ENTER THE NEW NEGRO

THE MARCH WAS ON! Blacks from all walks of life were strutting, vest buttons bursting, with optimism. This emerging era was the Age of the "New Negro," and it promised new opportunity and respect for blacks in America. Critic Alain Locke described this new way of thinking in his essay "Enter the New Negro," which was included in the celebrated March 1925 issue of *Survey Graphic*. Here, Locke makes the distinction between how African Americans used to be viewed and how that view was changing.

75

## HARLEM JIVE

from
*The Harlem Renaissance:
A Historical Dictionary
for the Era*

**Ah-ah.** A fool.

**Ain't got 'em.** Has no virtue; is of no value.

**Bardacious.** Wonderful; marvelous.

**Belly rub.** Sexy dance.

**Berries.** An expression of approval, as in, "She's the berries."

**Boogie-woogie.** A kind of dancing.

**Bookooing.** Showing off (from *beaucoup*).

**Bottle it, bottle et.** Shut up.

**Brick-presser.** An idler.

**Bring mud.** To disappoint.

**Buckra.** A white person.

**Bull-skating.** Bragging.

**Bump, bumpty-bump, bump the bump.** A slow, one-step dance.

**Catch the air.** To leave under pressure.

**Chip.** To steal.

**Cloakers.** Deceivers; liars.

**Collar a hot.** To eat a meal.

**Collar a nod.** To sleep.

**Cut.** To do something well.

[F]or generations in the mind of America, the Negro has been more of a formula than a human being — a something to be argued about, condemned or defended, to be "kept down," or "in his place," or "helped up," to be worried with or worried over, harassed or patronized, a social bogey or a social burden. . . . His shadow, so to speak, has been more real to him than his personality. Though having had to appeal from the unjust stereotypes of his oppressors and traducers to those of his liberators, friends and benefactors he has had to subscribe to the traditional positions from which his case has been viewed. Little true social or self-understanding has or could come from such a situation. . . .

Therefore the Negro to-day wishes to be known for what he is, even in his faults and shortcomings, and scorns a craven and precarious survival at the price of seeming to be what he is not. He resents being spoken of as a social ward or minor, even by his own, and to being regarded as a chronic patient for the sociological clinic, the sick man of American Democracy. . . .

And certainly, if in our lifetime the Negro should not be able to celebrate his full initiation into American democracy, he can at least, on the warrant of these things, celebrate the attainment of a significant and satisfying new phase of group development, and with it a spiritual Coming of Age.

As Locke and others spoke of a "renewed race-spirit that consciously and proudly sets itself apart," the community of Harlem as a whole went about celebrating the coming of this new age. In every corner of life — from kitchen mechanics to heiresses, from laborers to poets, from pot wrestlers to preachers — the vibe was hot. No matter what came down the road, they were optimistic that everything was going to be all right.

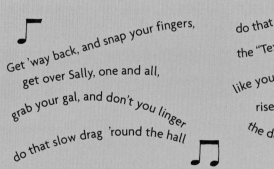

Get 'way back, and snap your fingers,
get over Sally, one and all,
grab your gal, and don't you linger
do that slow drag 'round the hall
do that step,
the "Texas Tommy" drop,
like you're sitting on a log,
rise slow, that will show,
the dance called the dog.

— from "Walkin' the Dog" by Shelton Brooks, 1916

## "TOO TERRIBLE PARTY"

O N ALMOST EVERY block in the poorer sections of town a tradition that originated in Southern cities became "Harlemized" — the rent party. The rents in Harlem were outrageous. By the mid-1920s a Harlem apartment could rent for as much as $25 a month *more* than a similar place in another section of the city. For blacks, that meant sometimes spending more than half one's salary on rent. The solution was not taking on another job, as most had done in the past. Instead, people would throw parties and charge admission to raise the extra money. Apartment dwellers throwing a rent party could expect to make $25 ($257 in today's dollars) from a hundred guests each paying twenty-five cents admission, as well as money from selling sandwiches and alcohol. After paying for the piano player, chair and piano rental, and food, the hosts were able to put away a sizeable nut toward that month's rent. This creative kind of problem solving represented a seismic change in attitude. A marvelous description of "what to do when the rent comes due" was published in Charles S. Johnson's anthology *Ebony and Topaz*. "Mrs. Bailey Pays the Rent," by Ira De A. Reid, offers a glimpse of a typical rent party.

There has been an evolution in the eclat of the rent party since it has become "Harlemized." The people have seen a new light, and are no longer wont to have it go unnamed. They called it a "Parlor Social." That term, however, along with "Rent Party" is for the spoken word. "Social Whist Party" looks much better in print and has become the prevailing terminology. Nor is its name restricted to these. Others include "Social Party," "Too Terrible Party," "Too Bad Party," "Matinee Party," "Parlor Social," "Whist Party," and "Social Entertainment."

There straggles along the cross-town streets of North Harlem a familiar figure. A middle aged white man, bent from his labor as the Wayside Printer, is pushing a little cart which has all of the equipment necessary for setting up the rent party ticket. The familiar tinkle of his bell in the late afternoon brings the representative of some family to his side. While you wait, he sets up your invitation with the bally-ho heading desired, and at a very reasonable price. The grammar and the English may be far from correct, but they meet all business requirements since they bring results. What work the Wayside printer does not get goes to the nearest print shop; some of which specialize in these announcements.

A true specimen of the popular mind is expressed in these tickets. The heading may be an expression from a popular song, a slang phrase, a theatrical quip or "poetry." A miscellaneous selection gives us the following: "Come and Get it Fixed"; "Leaving Me Papa, It's Hard To Do Because mam Done Put That Thing On You"; "If You Can't Hold Your Man, Don't Cry After He's Gone, Find Another"; "Clap Your Hands Here

---

**H U R R A Y**

COME AND SEE WHAT IS IN STORE FOR YOU AT THE

# TEA CUP PARTY

GIVEN BY MRS. VANDERBILT SMITH

at 409 EDGECOMBE AVENUE
NEW YORK CITY

Apartment 10-A

on Thursday evening, January 23rd, 1930

*at 8:00 P.M.*

ORIENTAL · GYPSY · SOUTHERN MAMMY ·
STARLIGHT
and other readers will be present

Music and Talent　　—　　—　　Refreshments Served

---

Fall in line, and watch your step, For there'll be
Lots of Browns with plenty of Pep At

*A Social Whist Party*

Given by

## Lucille & Minnie

149 West 117th Street, N.Y. Gr. floor, W,

**Saturday Evening, Nov. 2nd 1929**

Refreshments Just It　　　　　Music Won't Quit

---

If Sweet Mamma is running wild, and you are looking
for a Do-right child, just come around and
linger awhile at a

## SOCIAL WHIST PARTY

GIVEN BY

### PINKNEY & EPPS

260 West 129th Street　　　　　Apartment 10

**SATURDAY EVENING, JUNE 9, 1928**

GOOD MUSIC　　　　　REFRESHMENTS

---

*Railroad Men's Ball*

AT CANDY'S PLACE

*FRIDAY, SATURDAY & SUNDAY,*

*April 29-30, May 1, 1927*

Black Wax, says change your mind and say they
do and he will give you a hearing, while MEAT
HOUSE SLIM, laying in the bin
killing all good men.

L.A. VAUGH, *President*

Comes Charlie and He's Bringing Your Dinah Too"; "Old Uncle Joe, the Jelly Roll King is Back in Town and is Shaking That Thing"; "Here I am Again. Who? Daddy Jelly Roll and His Jazz Hounds"; "It's Too Bad Jim, But if You Want To Find a Sweet Georgia Brown, Come to the House of Mystery"; "You Don't Get Nothing for Being an Angel Child, So you Might as Well Get Real Busy and Real Wild".

And at various parties we find features, among them being "Music by the Late Kidd Morgan"; "Music by Kid Professor, the Father of the Piano"; "Music by Blind Johnny"; "Music by Kip Lippy"; "Skinny At the Traps"; "Music Galore"; "Charge De Affairs Bessie and Estelle"; "Here You'll Hear that Sweet Story That's Never Been Told"; "Refreshments to Suits"; "Refreshments by 'The Cheater'". All of these present to the average rent party habitueé a very definite picture of what is to be expected, as the card is given to him on the street corner, or at the subway station.

The parties outdo their publicity. There is always more than has been announced on the public invitation. Though no mention was made of an admission fee, one usually pays from twenty-five to fifty cents for this privilege. The refreshments are not always refreshing, but are much the same as those served in parts of the South, with gin and day-old Scotch extra. The Father of the Piano lives up to his reputation as he accompanies a noisy trap drummer, or a select trio composed of fife, guitar, and saxophone.

Apart from the admission fee and the sale of food, and drinks, the general tenor of the party is about the same as one would find in a group of "intellectual liberals" having a good time. Let us look at one. We arrived a little early — about nine-thirty o'clock. The ten persons present were dancing to the strains of the Cotton Club Orchestra via radio. The drayman was just bringing two dozen chairs from a nearby undertakers establishment, who rents them for such affairs. The hostess introduced herself, asked our names, and politely informed us that the "admittance fee" was thirty-five cents, which we paid. We were introduced to all, the hostess not remembering a single name. Ere the formality was over, the musicians, a piano player, saxophonist, and drummer, had arrived and immediately the party took on life. We learned that the saxophone player had been in big time vaudeville; that he could make his instrument "cry"; that he had quit the stage to play for the parties because he wanted to stay in New York.

So you Might as Well Get Real Busy and Real Wild."

"You Don't Get Nothing for Being an Angel Child,

79

A *New York Age* editorial
## RENT PARTY TRAGEDY
One of these rent parties a few weeks ago was the scene of a tragic crime in which one jealous woman cut the throat of another, because the two were rivals for the affections of a third woman. The whole situation was on a par with the recent Broadway play, imported from Paris, although the underworld tragedy took place in this locality. — In the meantime, the combination of bad gin, jealous women, a carving knife, and a rent party is dangerous to all health concerned.

"Muddy Water, round my feet — ta-ta-ta-ta-ta-ta.

There were more men than women, so a poker game was started in the next room, with the woman who did not care to dance, dealing. The music quickened the dancers. They say "Muddy Water, round my feet — ta-ta-ta-ta-ta-ta-ta". One girl remarked — "Now that party's getting right." The hostess informed us of the main menu of the evening — Pig feet and Chili — Sandwiches a la carte, and of course if your were thirsty, there was some "good stuff" available. Immediately, there was a rush to the kitchen, where the man of the house served your order.

For the first time we noticed a man who made himself conspicuous by his watchdog attitude toward all of us. He was the "Home Defense Officer," a private detective who was there to forestall any outside interference, as well as prevent any losses on the inside on account of the activity of the "Clean-up Men." There were two clean-up men there that night and the H.D.O. had to be particularly careful lest they walk away with two or three fur coats or some of the household furnishings. Sometimes these men would be getting the "lay" of the apartment for a subsequent visit.

There was nothing slow about this party. Perfect strangers at nine o'clock were boon companions at eleven. The bedroom had become the card room — a game of "skin" was in progress on the floor while dice rolled on the bed. There was something "shady" about the dice game, for one of the players was always having his dice caught. The musicians were still exhorting to the fifteen or twenty couples that danced. Bedlam reigned. It stopped for a few minutes while one young man hit another for getting fresh with his girl while dancing. The H.D.O. soon ended the fracas.

About two o'clock, a woman from the apartment on the floor below rang the bell and vociferously demanded that this noise stop or that she would call an officer. The hostess laughed in her face and slammed the door. Some tenants are impossible! This was sufficient however, to call the party to a halt. The spirit — or "spirits" had been dying by degrees. Everybody was tired — some had "dates" — others were sleepy — while a few wanted to make a caberet before "curfew hour." Mrs. Bailey calmly surveyed a disarranged apartment, and counted her proceeds.

And so the rent party goes on.

AME Zion Church

## KEEPING THE FAITH

BEFORE 1920 THE church was the center of all social activity among African Americans. With the coming of the renaissance and the economic boom, the church's influence declined but still remained a powerful resource for Harlem's middle class. By 1928 there were more than 160 African-American churches in Harlem, a result of the Great Migration in which people came North and brought their churches with them. As well, spiritualists of all kinds set up shop in storefronts, rented halls, parlors, and auditoriums. Among the more exotic were groups such as the Commandment Keepers, Holy Church of the Living God, the Pillar and Ground of Truth, the Temple of the Gospel of the Kingdom, the Metaphysical Church of the Divine Investigation, Prophet Bess, St. Matthew's Church of Divine Silence and Truth, Tabernacle of the Congregation of the Kingdom, and the Church of the Temple of Love.

From the most stable institutions to the most fly-by-night operations, these churches were not simply a place of worship. They provided a stabilizing force in a community that was experiencing an incredible influx of new people. The churches welcomed these

## BAREFOOT PROPHET

Through the coldest nights of winter and the hottest days of summer the Barefoot Prophet strode the streets of Harlem carrying the "Word." A giant of a man with huge feet and a magnificent mane of gray hair and a flowing beard, the Prophet often showed up at gin mills, cabarets, and rent parties, where he would quote a few passages of scripture, take up a small collection, and disappear into the night. According to legend, at an early age the Barefoot Prophet, whose real name was Elder Clayhorn Martin, had a vision in which God told him to "take off your shoes, for this is Holy Ground, Go preach My Gospel." He obeyed.

## FATHER DIVINE

The most bombastic of the cult churches at the time was the one known as the Righteous Government, lead by a man called Father Divine. His followers referred to him as "God," and they often renamed themselves a panoply of odd names, such as Pearly Gates, Beauty Smiles, Norah Endurance, Holy Shinelight, and Rose Memory. The church itself was famous for the free meals it offered to all comers.

newcomers with open arms and offered them an instant social life. They served as social centers, supplied relief to the orphaned and aged, promoted educational and cultural activities, initiated many civil rights actions, and offered an exclusively black point of view. At the center of all this was the clergy, who acted as part politician and part social worker, part moral counselor and part employment agent. In short, the clergy were involved in almost every aspect of their parishioners' lives.

Within this community African Americans who were pigeonholed in dead-end jobs could come to church on Sunday and regain their self-respect. Most large Harlem churches would open early on Sunday morning and remain open until ten or eleven o'clock at night. Parishioners would spend the entire day there, taking meals in the rectory and attending meetings and services. Churchgoing meant dressing in one's "Sunday best," forgetting for a time about work, meeting others, and attending to spiritual affairs. The fact that there were so many churches testified to the real need the average African American had for an affordable place to socialize without restrictions.

St. Phillips
Episcopal Church.

## THOSE JUST-SO SOIREES

**Diddy-wah-diddy.** A far-distant place; a measure of distance.

**Dickty.** Swell; grand; high-toned.

**Dig.** To understand.

**Dog.** Used as a complimentary noun, as in, "Ain't this a dog?"

**Dog it.** To show off; to strut; as to "put on the dog."

**Dog mah cats.** An expression of astonishment.

**Dogging.** Dancing.

**Doing the dozens.** In verbal agreement, to insult another person's parents.

**Down to the bricks.** To the limit.

**Fooping.** Fooling around.

**Frail eel.** A pretty girl.

**Fungshun.** A crowded dance with too many people smelling of sweat (a play on *function*).

**Gum beater.** A braggart or idle talker.

**Gut bucket.** A sleazy cabaret; also: racous, vulgar music.

**Hincty.** Snooty.

**Hot.** Wonderful; marvelous.

HARLEM SPORTED MORE than 700 social clubs, which sponsored activities ranging from noisy "chitterlin' suppers" and "barrel house" parties to stilted soirees, symposiums, and musicales. The more rarefied of these clubs strived for a social correctness that mirrored that of its downtown white counterparts. The formal winter season began on Thanksgiving eve and ran until the beginning of Lent. One of the most fashionable events of this season was the Alpha Bowling Club ball. The Alpha Club was a charity organization, but it spent most of its time putting on formal events. The guest lists included the most respected individuals of the community — Harlem's schoolteachers, businesspeople, undertakers, nurses, post office employees, physicians, dentists, lawyers, and a small group of dignified domestics who had long been employed by New York's white aristocracy.

Harlem Bridge Club meeting

### LA BOURGEOISIE NOIRE

E. Franklin Frazier, a professor of sociology at Howard University, coined the term "La Bourgeoisie Noire" to describe the business class of Harlem. These were the people who escaped the white man's kitchen and dining room. They were made up of families of professional men — doctors, lawyers, and ministers — along with judges, actors, "race leaders," politicians, educators, and moneyed prize fighters. On the whole these upper-class families embraced a conservative taste and a deep sense of respectability.

## LET'S HAVE A PARADE!

Harlem is also a parade ground. During the warmer months of the year no Sunday passes without several parades. There are brass bands, marchers in resplendent regalia, and high dignitaries with gorgeous insignia riding in automobiles. Almost any excuse for parading is sufficient — the funeral of a member of the lodge, laying of a corner-stone, the annual sermon to the order, or just a general desire to "turn out." Parades are not limited to Sunday; for when the funeral of a lodge member falls on a weekday, it is quite the usual thing to hold the exercises at night, so that members of the order and friends who are at work during the day may attend. Frequently after nightfall a slow procession may be seen wending its way along and a band heard playing a dirge that takes on a deeply sepulchral tone. But generally these parades are lively and add greatly to the movement, colour, and gaiety of Harlem. A brilliant parade with very good bands is participated in not only by the marcher in line, but also by the marchers on the sidewalks. For it is not a universal custom of Harlem to stand idly and watch a parade go by; a good part of the crowd always marches along, keeping step to the music.

— James Weldon Johnson, from *Black Manhattan*

Funeral procession on Seventh Ave.

For the college-educated, all the national African-American fraternities and sororities had New York chapters. Although the majority of their work involved race issues, scholarships, and donations to African-American social agencies, these groups sponsored full social programs and demanded of their members a code of conduct similar to that of elite white social clubs. One fraternity advised its brothers in advance of its annual convention as follows:

> Clothing for the formal affairs — late August is likely to be moderately warm in New York City. The type of formal wear is left optional with the Brothers. They can wear either tuxedos or various types of summer formal apparel. However, in all cases **FORMAL APPAREL** must be worn — **NO WHITE LINEN SUITS** are considered formal attire.

Charlotte van der Veer Quick Mason

## NEGROTARIANS

Zora Neale Hurston labeled the many whites who helped finance and support the Harlem Renaissance "Negrotarians." These white patrons had only their color in common, since their reasons for involvement ranged from social interest to a belief that blacks were victims of civil rights abuses to an interest in recruiting blacks for revolutionary political purposes. Carl Van Vechten was one of the most prominent white patrons. Countee Cullen wrote the poem "For a Lady I Know" about one of the most notorious "Negrotarians," Charlotte van der Veer Quick Mason. Known to her beneficiaries as "Godmother," she was enormously rich and believed in her twilight years that true spirituality existed only in primitive people. She insisted that her "godchildren" sit at her feet and often demanded that they beg for money.

**Jive.** To pursue; to capture; to deceive; also: slang talk; black music.

**Jump salty.** To get angry.

**Kitchen mechanic.** A domestic servant or laborer.

**Kopasetee.** A term of approval (from *copasetic*).

**Mug man.** A small-time criminal or thug.

**Negrotarian.** A white do-gooder, coined by Zora Neale Hurston.

**Oscar.** A stupid person.

**Piano.** Spareribs.

**Pole out.** To be distinguished or excel.

**Rug-cutter.** A person too cheap to frequent dance halls who goes to rent parties and proceeds to "cut up" the rugs of the house with his hot feet; also: a good dancer.

**Shim sham shimmy.** An erotic dance.

**Shout.** A ball or prom; also: a one-step dance.

**Slip, slip in the dozens.** To joke with or to kid either one person or a whole group.

**Smoking over.** Looking over critically.

## STROLLING

Strolling is almost a lost art in New York; at least, in the manner in which it is so generally practiced in Harlem. Strolling in Harlem does not mean merely walking along Lenox or upper Seventh Avenue or One Hundred and Thirty-fifth Street; it means that those streets are places for socializing. One puts on one's best clothes and fares forth to pass the time pleasantly with the friends and acquaintances and, most important of all, the strangers he is sure of meeting. One saunters along, he hails this one, exchanges a word or two with that one, stops for a short chat with the other one. He comes up to a laughing, chattering group, in which he may have only one friend or acquaintance, but that gives him the privilege of joining in. He does join in and takes part in the joking, the small talk and gossip, and makes new acquaintances. . . . This is not simply going out for a walk; it is more like going out for an adventure.

— James Weldon Johnson, from *Black Manhattan*

"Man, we strolled in Harlem. This was our turf."

— Elton Fox

**Solid.** Perfect.

**Sooner.** Cheap or shabby.

**Stomp.** A raucous dance party.

**Stroll.** To do something well, as in, "He's really strolling."

**Syndicating.** Gossiping.

**Trucking.** To walk with style; also: a dance step resembling the stroll.

**Wobble.** A dance.

**Woofing.** Gossip; casual or aimless talk.

**Work under cork.** To appear on stage in blackface makeup.

# FROM THE DARK TOWER

The night whose sable breast relieves the stark,

White stars is no less lovely being dark,

And there are buds that cannot bloom at all

In light, but crumple, piteous, and fall . . .

— COUNTEE CULLEN

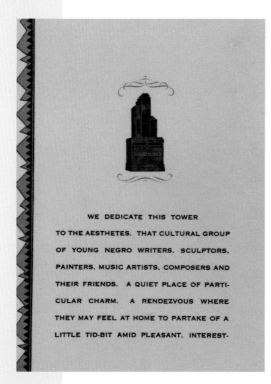

WE DEDICATE THIS TOWER TO THE AESTHETES. THAT CULTURAL GROUP OF YOUNG NEGRO WRITERS. SCULPTORS. PAINTERS. MUSIC ARTISTS. COMPOSERS AND THEIR FRIENDS. A QUIET PLACE OF PARTICULAR CHARM. A RENDEZVOUS WHERE THEY MAY FEEL AT HOME TO PARTAKE OF A LITTLE TID-BIT AMID PLEASANT. INTEREST-

L IKE THE LINES from Cullen's sonnet "From the Dark Tower," Harlem flourished in darkness bathed in moonlight. Most official events, including funerals, were held at night, when those who held jobs were off. The most lavish of these moon-lit events were the parties thrown by A'Lelia Walker — *the* hostess of the Harlem Renaissance. Walker was the heiress to Madam C. J. Walker's hair-straightening empire, which sold "Madam Walker's Wonderful Hair Grower" and invented a process to take the tight curls, or "kink," out of the hair of black women. A'Lelia Walker was a striking woman who stood six feet tall and dressed to emphasize her size with high heels and tall, plumed headdresses and turbans. Throughout the 1920s, the Walker fortune financed hundreds of parties where blacks and whites alike socialized, only to end when A'Lelia Walker died in 1931.

A'Lelia Walker's most famous contribution to the scene was the establishment of a literary salon — the Dark Tower — in 1928. The name was taken from the title of Countee Cullen's monthly column in *Opportunity*. Inspired by her bohemian friends, Walker planned to have music and dancing on one floor of her mansion at 108–110 West 136th Street, while in the library on another floor African-American art would be displayed and poetry would be read.

Dubbed the "de-kink heiress," Walker relished in her extravaganzas and invited not just the "upper rungs of the sepia social ladder," but also downtown's white "society café" crowd, Broadway stars, jazz luminaries, and even royalty. Guests would pass through ornate French doors, walk down a hallway with a blue velvet runner, and enter a magnificently decorated tearoom, where Langston Hughes's poem "The Weary Blues" was stenciled on the wall. For fifteen cents guests could check their hats and ogle the talking parrot. Here, the champagne flowed and the music was hot. Someone was always on the Knabe baby grand piano while Broadway stars such as Alberta Hunter, Adelaide Hall, and the Four Bon Bons performed.

The Dark Tower and other social events like it gave African Americans the opportunity to stand above whites by making them come uptown to their community. The implications of this was that whites would have to learn to fit in with blacks, and not the other way around.

Geraldyn Dismond, society reporter for the black *Interstate Tattler,* vividly described one of the Dark Tower gatherings:

A'Lelia Walker

What a crowd! All classes and colors met face to face, ultra aristocrats, Bourgeois, Communists, Park Avenue galore, bookers, publishers, Broadway celebs, Harlemites giving each other the once over. The social revolution was on. And yes, Lady Nancy Cunard was there all in black (she would) with twelve of her grand bracelets. . . . And was the entertainment on the up and up! Into swell dance music was injects of African drums that played havoc with blood pressure. Jimmy Daniels and his gigilo hits, Gus Simons, the Harlem crooner, made the "River Stay Away From His Door" and Taylor himself brought out everything from "Hot Dog" to "Bravo" when he made high C.

*Interpretation of Harlem Jazz*, 1925, Winold Reiss.

# STOMPIN'
## AT THE SAVOY

**MUSIC AND DANCE OF THE RENAISSANCE**

Put it this way. Jazz is a good barometer of freedom.

— DUKE ELLINGTON

## THE JAM

THE PARTY WAS ON, and Harlem was at the center of what F. Scott Fitzgerald came to call "The Jazz Age." And the Harlem speakeasy was the epicenter of it all because that's where the jazz was. Blaring trumpets, hot clarinets, and booming drums could be heard up and down Lexington Avenue. These sounds called people from the streets to come in, brush off their troubles, and dance! In the 1920s, jazz was dance music that made your foot tap and your hips sway. It was an exuberant, carefree music with a driving rhythm and a blistering melody. It was the kind of music that speakeasy owners loved because it kept customers dancing — which guaranteed they'd work up a giant thirst. (Speakeasies were places that sold alcohol illegally.)

91

## HARLEM'S JAZZ GENIUSES

### LOUIS "SATCHMO" ARMSTRONG, 1900–1971

LOUIS ARMSTRONG got his nickname "Satchmo" because he had a big mouth. As a child he was first called "Dippermouth" and then "Satchelmouth," which later morphed into a shortened "Satchmo." In the 1920s, Armstrong changed the ensemble nature of jazz and turned it into a soloist's art. He played so loudly and so uniquely that he single-handedly invented the improvised solo, while his vocal stylizations exhibited a new kind of rhythmic elasticity, called scat, that revolutionized jazz singing. Recordings such as *The Last Time* (1927), *I Can't Give You Anything But Love* (1929), and *Heebie Jeebies* (1926) created a whole new kind of jazz in the twenties.

### DUKE ELLINGTON, 1899–1974

EDWARD KENNEDY ELLINGTON moved to New York from Washington, D.C., to study art at the Pratt Institute, but it was jazz that lured him out of the classroom and into nightclubs. In 1918 he organized his own jazz band, and during the 1920s he performed regularly at all of Harlem's hottest clubs, including five years at the famous Cotton Club. His influence was tremendous as a pianist, composer, and conductor. More than any other musician at the time, Ellington expanded on the narrowly conceived formalism of jazz to make it broader and more open-ended.

"Louis Armstrong's overwhelming message is one of love. When you hear his music, it's of joy. . . . He was just not going to be defeated by the forces of life."

— Wynton Marsalis, jazz trumpeter

**A Selection from Langston Hughes's
100 Favorite Recordings,**
*The First Book of Jazz*

**Back Water Blues**
Bessie Smith
Columbia (1927)

**Christopher Columbus**
Fletcher Henderson
Decca (1936)

**Dippermouth Blues**
King Oliver's Creole Jazz Band
Brunswick (1923)

**I'm Gonna Sit Right Down
and Write Myself a Letter**
Fats Waller
Victor (1935)

**Minnie the Moocher**
Cab Calloway
Brunswick (1930)

**Memphis Blues and Others**
W. C. Handy
Audio Archives (1912)

**St. Louis Blues**
Louis Armstrong
Okeh (1929)

**The Mooche**
Duke Ellington
Victor (1928)

# TEN BASIC ELEMENTS OF JAZZ

**From *The First Book of Jazz* by Langston Hughes**

**SYNCOPATION** This is a shifting of the normal rhythmic stress from the strong beat to the weak beat, accenting the offbeat, and playing one rhythm against another in such a way that listeners want to move, nod heads, clap hands, or dance. Syncopation is basic and continuous in jazz, and upon it are built very complex rhythms.

**IMPROVISATION** This is composing as one plays, or making up variations on old themes directly on the instrument being played rather than from written notes. The interest and beauty of improvisation depends on the talent and the ability of the individual performer.

**PERCUSSION** The drums provide jazz with its basic beat, but the banjo or guitar, the string bass or tuba, and the piano also provide percussion. Any or all of these instruments may make up the rhythm section of a jazz band. Chords may be used as a beat to create harmonized percussion.

**RHYTHM** In jazz this is not limited to percussion beats alone. The variations of volume, tone, and pitch may also be used in such a way as to give to a jazz performance additional accents of sound-rhythm, played against a variety of counter-rhythms supplied by the percussion.

**BLUE NOTES** These are glissando or slurred notes, somewhere between flat and natural, derived from the blues as sung, and sliding into intervals between major and minor. Blue notes are impossible to notate exactly, but when written down on paper they are frequently indicated by the flatted third or seventh notes of the scale.

**TONE COLOR** Jazz instruments may take on the varied tones of the singing or speaking voice, even of laughter or of groans, in a variety of tonal colorations. At one time different instruments may be playing different melodies.

**HARMONY** In jazz, harmony makes frequent use of the blue note, the blue scale, the seventh and ninth chords, and the "close" harmony of the old barbershop style of chromatic singing, which is carried over into instrumentation.

**BREAK** This is a very brief syncopated interlude, usually of two to four bars, between musical phrases — often improvised in unwritten jazz. Armstrong is famous for his breaks.

**RIFF** This is a single rhythmic phrase repeated over and over, usually as a background to the lead melody. A riff may be used also as a melodic theme in itself.

**JOY OF PLAYING** This is the element that gives jazz its zest and verve, its happy, dancing quality, that brings musicians of all races together in impromptu jam sessions. Here new musical ideas are born as the musicians play together for hours without written music — just for fun.

## CUTTING CONTESTS

JAMES P. JOHNSON, "the Father of Stride Piano," Willie "the Lion" Smith, and Thomas "Fats" Waller were just three of the great stride pianists of the twenties who specialized in what they called "orchestral piano," which featured expressive, widespread chords juxtaposing the left hand's loping style with the right hand's melody. After gigs, these and other striders would produce dazzling up-tempo pyrotechnics on the piano as they competed in ferocious late-night cutting contests. William Henry Joseph Bonaparte Bertholoff Smith, better known as Willie "the Lion" Smith, described these contests:

Fats Waller

> Sometimes we got carving battles going that would last for four or five hours. We would embroider the melodies with our own original ideas and try to develop patterns that had more originality than those played before us. Sometimes it was just a question of who could think up the most patterns within a given tune. It was pure improvisation. You had to have your own individual style and be able to play in all the keys. In those days we could all copy each other's shouts by learning them by ear. Sometimes, in order to keep the others from picking up too much of my stuff, I'd perform in the hard keys, B major and E major.

In these competitions striders would perform their most difficult and complex arrangements to see who was top dog. Only the most nimble hands survived these lightning-quick competitions.

"It was pure improvisation."

— Willie "the Lion" Smith

95

"At the Savoy Ballroom, social, racial, and economic proble

**THE STOMP**

Jazz wasn't just music. It was music to dance to. Harlem nightclubs were the center of all the new steps — the Charleston, the lindy hop, the black bottom, truckin', snakehips, the break, and more. This illustration by Miguel Covarrubias is of two dancers doing the lindy hop, one of Harlem's dances that caught fire across America.

## OPENING NIGHT AT THE SAVOY BALLROOM

WITHOUT QUESTION THE Savoy was the hottest, wildest, and most integrated dance club in Harlem — "The Home of Happy Feet." On opening night, March 12, 1927, four thousand people — from kitchen mechanics to the Talented Tenth to white café society — descended to "trip the light fantastic," to clap hands to the Charleston, to truck around the dance floor, and to swing out doing the ballroom's own lindy hop. It was the lindy that morphed into the swing era's jitterbug.

The Savoy Ballroom, a low, white stucco building, spanned an entire block along Lenox Avenue between 140th and 141st Streets. Patrons entered through a pair of double doors into a grand lobby dominated by a huge, cut-glass chandelier.

Patrons paid from forty cents to a dollar to enter, ascended a mirrored stairwell up two flights, and were greeted by the rhythm of a big band. The music bounced across the blocklong dance floor — 50 feet wide and 250 feet long. At one end stood a raised bandstand. Unlike most dance clubs, the Savoy had two bandstands so that the music never stopped between sets. On opening night Fess Williams, cut in a diamond- and ruby- studded suit, led his Royal Flush Orchestra out onto the bandstand. Williams blew a hot reed on his clarinet while his band played driving jazz with a heavy rhythm. Later that evening the Savoy Bearcats swung into the groove, and after midnight Fletcher Henderson and his Rainbow Orchestra blew the doors off the place.

de away to nothingness."

— *Amsterdam News*

Over the next few years the biggest names in big-band jazz would set the dance rhythms at the Savoy — Louis Armstrong, Cab Calloway, Duke Ellington, Fess Williams, Chick Webb, and King Oliver.

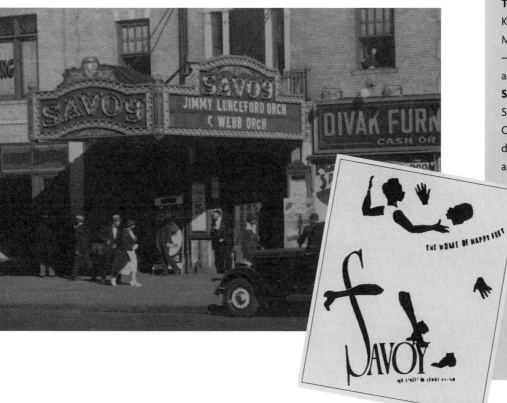

**THE SAVOY'S WEEKLY SPECIALS**

**TUESDAY**
The 400 Club — only serious dancers allowed.

**THURSDAY**
Kitchen Mechanics Night — ladies admitted free.

**SATURDAY**
Square's Night Out — white downtowners and wannabes.

**SUNDAY**
Glamour Night — movie stars, performers, and selected international elite.

**"Out on the dance floor, everyone, dickty and rat, rubbed joyous elbows, laughing, mingling, forgetting differences, but whenever the music stopped everyone immediately sought their own level."**

— Rudolf Fisher on the Savoy Ballroom

97

## HARLEMANIA

B Y THE MID-TWENTIES Harlem was the place to be for nightlife, and it remained that way until the Wall Street crash in 1929. A love of everything Harlem was just about everywhere, from the all-black Broadway revues downtown to Paris's hot jazz bands. Harlem was on everyone's mind — even whites, and not only the white supporters of the renaissance's literature but also trendsetters such as Princess Violette Murat, Mayor James J. Walker, Lady Mountbatten, and screen star Harold Lloyd. It was fashionable to have played in the nightclubs and cabarets of Harlem. That did not mean, however, that whites wanted to socialize with blacks as equals. Consequently, a whole industry of white clubs arose, offering black exotica at a distance. These were the Jim Crow night-clubs in the heart of Harlem.

Gangster Owney "The Killer" Madden, one of the most notorious criminals of the era, presided over the most famous of these establishments — the Cotton Club. Located on 142nd Street near Lenox Avenue, the Cotton Club opened in 1923, shortly after Madden completed a prison sentence for murder. Ironically, white socialites felt more comfortable rubbing elbows with a murderer than with the black working class.

The Cotton Club had a log cabin exterior and interior and featured jungle décor. Bandleader Cab Calloway, who first performed there in 1930, described the club:

**The bandstand was a replica of a southern mansion with large white columns and a backdrop painted with weeping willows and slave quarters. . . . The waiters were dressed in red tuxedos, like butlers in a southern mansion, and . . . there were huge cut-crystal chandeliers.**

Once inside, white revelers could do the Charleston on the dance floor and watch the all-black revues from the safe distance of their café tables. The entertainment featured an extravagant mix of dancing, vaudeville, and the great Duke Ellington and his orchestra. These shows would often last for at least two hours, which was more on the level of a Broadway show than a nightclub performance.

At the Cotton Club the chorus line was composed exclusively of "high yaller" female dancers who were under twenty-one years of age and over five feet six inches.

In a still from a 1929 motion picture called *Black and Tan*, Duke Ellington and his orchestra preside over a stage show at the Cotton Club.

"The chief ingredient was pace, pace, pace! The show was generally built around types: the band, an eccentric dancer, a comedian — whoever we had who was also a star. . . . And we'd have a special singer who gave the customers the expected adult song in Harlem."

— Dan Healy, singer, dancer, comic, and producer of the Cotton Club shows

"Got the world in a jug, got the stopper in my hand."

— Bessie Smith, "Down Hearted Blues"

**Variety's List of White Nightclubs in Harlem**

The Cotton Club

Connie's Inn

The Nest Club

Small's Paradise

Barron's

The Spider Web

The Saratoga Club

Ward's Swanee

Pod's and Jerry's Catagonia Club

The Bamboo Inn

The Lenox

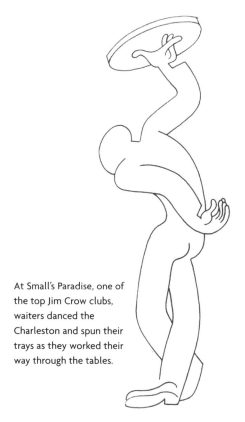

At Small's Paradise, one of the top Jim Crow clubs, waiters danced the Charleston and spun their trays as they worked their way through the tables.

With whites taking the A train uptown in unprecedented numbers, blacks felt exactly as Bessie Smith expressed in her classic blues song — that everything was under control. It did not matter that most whites were heading for the Jim Crow nightclubs from which blacks were excluded, because it was *their* music and *their* performers that the "ofays" came to see. ("Ofay" was a derogatory term based on the pig latin of "foe" and used by blacks to describe whites.) Harlemites reveled in this magnificent change in status after years of having been at best ignored and at worst lynched, but they didn't overlook the fact that they were not being invited downtown. Many believed that the acceptance of jazz and the increased visibility of black culture were just the first steps in their becoming true citizens of the United States. For them, they had the stopper in their hand, and nobody was going to take it away.

African-American performer Bert Williams in black face.

**BLACKS AND THE AMERICAN THEATER**

We wear the mask that grins and lies.

— PAUL LAURENCE DUNBAR

## NO MORE MASKS

April 5, 1917, is the date of the most important single event in the entire history of the Negro in the American theatre; for it marks the beginning of a new era. On that date a performance of three dramatic plays was given by the Coloured Players at the Garden Theatre in Madison Square Garden, New York, and the stereotyped traditions regarding the Negro's histrionic limitations were smashed.

JAMES WELDON JOHNSON used this forceful language to describe three one-act plays written by white playwright Ridgely Torrence. What made Torrence's plays, *The Rider of Dreams, Granny Maumee,* and *Simon the Cyrenian,* so groundbreaking was the fact that they depicted African-American characters far removed from the "coons" of a minstrel show.

103

American theater had traditionally portrayed African Americans in an extremely narrow way that had no real connection to black culture and its music, dance, or arts. Two stereotypes — Jim Crow and Jim Dandy (or Zip Coon) — dominated the white stage. Jim Crow was the rough, coarse barbarian who wore tattered clothes. Jim Dandy was a slick urban fop, slightly feminine and dressed to the nines. Both of these characters were created and played by white actors who were "blacked up" with burnt cork. In short, African Americans were portrayed on stage as either comic or pathetic. Overall, the stock black character was childlike, lazy, slow moving, and a victim of his bodily appetites. He was all mouth, gullet, and stomach. In fact, minstrels even made themselves up with huge lips suggesting a cavernous mouth.

It was because of these bigoted depictions that Torrence's one-act plays had such a powerful effect on American theater. Critics hailed the plays' originality and even named two of the actors, Opal Cooper and Inex Clough, among the top-ten performers of the year. "Nobody who saw Opal Cooper — and heard him as the dream Madison Sparrow — will ever forget the lift his performance gave," wrote *Theatre Magazine*'s Edith Isaacs.

A drawing of Simon the Cyrenian made by Djuna Barnes to accompany her review of Ridgely Torrence's *Three Plays for a Negro Theatre.*

This breakthrough, however, did not last long. In fact, it hardly lasted twenty-four hours because the day after the plays opened, the United States declared war on Germany. It took three years and the end of World War I for another play involving blacks to be produced. White playwright Eugene O'Neill's *The Emperor Jones* opened at Greenwich Village's Provincetown Theatre in November 1920, and with it came the opportunity for blacks to portray complex characters. Charles Gilpin, who starred in *The Emperor Jones,* was hailed by *The New Republic* as one of the finest performers on the American stage. As well, he was awarded the 1921 Spingarn Medal for his outstanding performance.

In the 1920s, dramatic roles on the stage exploded for African Americans. The actor who epitomized the decade-long expansion of opportunities for black actors was Paul Robeson. In April of 1922 he made his first stage appearance in the play *Taboo*. Two years later Robeson starred in Eugene O'Neill's play *All God's Chillun Got Wings*, which is about an upper-class black man married to a poor white woman. When word got out that Robeson would be kissing a white actress on stage, an uproar arose with demands to ban the play for fear of riots. Nevertheless, the show went on, and nothing happened. Robeson went on to reprise Gilpin's role in the revival of *The Emperor Jones* in 1925, and he appeared in the Broadway musical *Showboat* (1928), singing the spiritual "Ol' Man River."

## PAUL ROBESON, 1898–1976

One of the most accomplished Americans of any race, Paul Robeson was a successful singer, actor, civil rights activist, lawyer, world-class athlete, scholar, and author. Born on April 9, 1898, in Princeton, New Jersey, Robeson excelled in both scholastics and athletics as a youth. He won a scholarship to Rutgers University, where he was elected to Phi Beta Kappa as a junior and was chosen valedictorian in his senior year. He was also an All-American football player. In the 1920s after graduating from law school, Robeson became one of the most celebrated and recognized African-American performers. He first joined the Provincetown Players and starred in a number of O'Neill's plays, including *The Emperor Jones* and *All God's Chillun Got Wings*; then he went on to earn international accolades for his performances. In 1925, however, Robeson embarked on a career as a solo vocal performer in which he sang spirituals and work songs to audiences of common citizens all over the world. He became best-known for his powerful, soothing rendition of "Ol' Man River" in the Broadway musical and subsequent film adaption of *Showboat*. Later in life, his achievements became overshadowed by his support of communism. At one point he was blacklisted in the United States and had his passport revoked. He spent the final years of his life as a pariah to much of the American public, but beloved in Europe. While overseas, Robeson wrote his now-acclaimed autobiography, *Here I Stand*, which major publications, including the *New York Times*, refused to review.

The stage set of *Porgy*.

THE THEATRE GUILD PRES

PORGY

REPUBLIC THEATRE
42 STREET WEST of BROADWAY

During the decade numerous plays were written and produced by whites that gave blacks an unprecedented opportunity to perform respectable, serious drama in downtown theaters. Some of the more celebrated plays included Paul Green's *Abraham's Bosom,* which won the Pulitzer Prize in 1926; Edward Sheldon and Charles MacArthur's *Lulu Belle* (1926); Torrence's *Granny Maumee* (1927); DuBose Heyward's *Mamba's Daughter* (1927); and DuBose and Dorothy Heyward's *Porgy* (1928), which was the inspiration for George Gershwin's acclaimed opera *Porgy and Bess*. The decade ended with the greatest commercial success — Marc Connelly's *The Green Pastures* (1930). However, perhaps more than any other production, *The Green Pastures* epitomized the white playwright's stereotypical portrayal of black naïveté.

**"If, north of 116th Street, conditions are as disorderly as William Jourdan Rapp and Wallace Thurman paint them, the white man's burden is, if possible, even heavier than it seems."**

Many black intellectuals were disappointed by these productions. First, these plays were written exclusively by whites about African-American life and were produced by whites for white audiences. Second, the portrayals of blacks in these productions were not as complex as they purported to be. Many of the roles were limited to the stereotype of childlike sentimentality that seemed no better than the minstrel stereotypes. Nevertheless, Harlem residents came to accept these shows at least for economic reasons. The plays featured large casts, which offered job opportunities much more rewarding than the usual labor jobs. In fact, such Harlem Renaissance luminaries as Wallace Thurman and Richarch Bruce Nugent were among the many extras hired for *Porgy*.

In 1898, *A Trip to Coontown* was the first theatrical show to be organized, written, produced, and managed by blacks.

The only black-authored drama to make it to Broadway during the decade was Wallace Thurman and William Rapp's *Harlem* in 1929. The African-American community, however, was a much harsher critic of its own, expecting black playwrights not to stoop to the tastes of white audiences. A critic for the Chicago *Defender* cracked, "If, north of 116th Street, conditions are as disorderly as William Jourdan Rapp and Wallace Thurman paint them, the white man's burden is, if possible, even heavier than it seems." The play *Harlem* explored the theme of prejudice against West Indians, but also continued to focus on the working-class elements of black culture, to the exasperation of W. E. B. Du Bois and other prominent middle-class African Americans.

"The funniest man I ever saw."

— comedian and film star W. C. Fields

### BERT WILLIAMS, 1875–1922

Born on March 11, 1875, in Antigua, West Indies, Egbert "Bert" Williams moved with his family to California when he was ten. As a young man he attended Stanford University, but he dropped out to perform in saloons in San Francisco. In 1893 Williams met George Walker, and together they formed the most famous comedy duo of the turn of the century. By 1901 they were the first African-American artists to record on disk. Their 1902 musical *In Dahomey* was a hit on Broadway and across Europe. By 1909, however, Walker had died, and Williams went on to a celebrated career as the only African American to star with the Ziegfield Follies on Broadway. Williams was noted for performing "blacked up," but somehow he transcended the "darkie" stereotype. In 1918 Williams described his theory behind comedy: "All the jokes in the world are based on a few elemental ideas. . . . Troubles are funny only when you pin them down to one particular individual. And that individual, the fellow who is the goat, must be the man who is singing the song or telling the story." Williams died in 1922 at the age of 47.

**"It is no disgrace to be a Negro, but it is very inconvenient."**

— Bert Williams

# SHUFFLING ALONG

WHILE WHITES CONTROLLED the legitimate theater, African Americans made headway in musicals — writing, producing, and performing them. The most important of these musicals was *Shuffle Along* (1921), which opened off Broadway on May 23, 1921, and was a huge box-office success. The music and dance in *Shuffle Along* set the tone for the Roaring Twenties. A New York *Herald* critic explained, "It is when the chorus and the principles . . . gets going in the dances that the world seems a brighter place to live in. They wriggle and shimmy in a fashion to outdo a congress of eels, and they fling their limbs about without stopping to make sure they are securely fastened on."

On the whole, *Shuffle Along* was hardly different from the old minstrel shows with darkie skits, blacked-up comedians, and mammy songs. The only difference was that blacks profited along with whites now because black actors were used. But the play was progressive in its music and dance. Written and scored by Eubie Blake and Noble Sissle, the music featured hot jazz and such classic songs as "I'm Just Wild About Harry" and "Love Will Find A Way," which became illustrative of the Jazz Age. The show also launched the careers of a number of future stars, including Florence Mills and Josephine Baker. Paul Robeson even made an appearance in the revue as a replacement cast member. *Shuffle Along* was emblematic of how the system had both changed for the better and the worse.

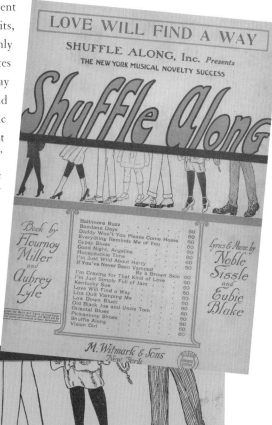

## Jazz Musicals of the Twenties

*Shuffle Along* (1921)

*Strut Miss Lizzie* (1922)

*Seven-Eleven* (1922)

*Liza* (1923)

*Runnin' Wild* (1923)

*How Come?* (1923)

*Dixie to Broadway* (1924)

*In Barnville* (1924)

*Chocolate Dandies* (1925)

*Lucky Sambo* (1925)

*My Magnolia* (1926)

*Blackbirds of 1926* (1926)

*Africana* (1927)

*Rang Tang* (1927)

*Bottomland* (1927)

*Keep Shufflin'* (1928)

*Blackbirds of 1928* (1928)

*Bamboola* (1929)

*Hot Chocolates* (1929)

Fats Waller, one of the finest jazz composers and musicians of the era, is reputed to have dashed off "Ain't Misbehavin'" in forty-five minutes. But, almost always broke, he sold it even faster. In a moment of desperation, he sold his rights to it, and to eighteen other songs, for $500 ($5,260 in today's dollars). Louis Armstrong introduced "Ain't Misbehavin'" in a 1929 Broadway revue, *Hot Chocolates*. It showed up again on Broadway in 1978 in *Ain't Misbehavin'*, a show composed of music associated with Waller.

## HARLEM DRAMA

THOSE CLOSEST TO the "New Negro" movement hungered for an authentic African-American theater that didn't play to stereotypes. These intellectuals recognized how on Broadway black identity was merely a projection of white perception and white needs — not their own. In these "stage negroes" they could not recognize themselves or their neighbors. Consequently, New Negro supporters became committed to establishing a theater experience constructed by, for, and about African Americans.

One of the earliest to speak out for a legitimate black theater was African-American playwright Willis Richardson. He wanted to see plays that captured the richness, diversity, and beauty of his race. As early as 1919 Richardson issued a call for a national Negro theater "able to send a company of Negro Players with Negro Plays across our own continent [and] . . . to the artistic peoples of Europe." During the twenties Richardson wrote six one-act plays anchored in a realism that represented ordinary blacks who suffered from their own weaknesses or society's shortcomings.

Richardson mapped out a program for creating serious African-American drama in four essays for *Opportunity* magazine. In "The Negro and the Stage" (October 1924), he argued that "theater should always, and seriously, be considered as an educational institution side by side with the school." His next essay, "The Negro Audience" (April 1925),

# AIN'T MISBEHAVIN'

Lyrics for the stage show *Hot Chocolates*, 1929.
Words by Andy Razaf. Music by Thomas "Fats" Waller
and Harry Brooks.

No one to walk with.
All by myself.
No one to talk with,
But I'm happy
On the shelf.
Ain't misbehavin',
I'm savin' my love for you.

I know for certain
The one I love.
I'm through with flirtin',
It's you that I'm thinkin' of.
Ain't misbehavin',
I'm savin' my love for you.

Like Jack Horner
In the corner.
Don't go nowhere.
What do I care?
Your kisses
Are worth waitin' for,
Believe me.

I don't stay out late,
Don't care to go.
I'm home about eight,
Just me and my radio.
Ain't misbehavin',
I'm savin' my love for you.

spelled out the key criteria necessary "if the Negro drama is to prosper and become 'a thing of beauty and a joy forever'; whether the characters are well drawn, whether the dialogue is natural, whether the ending is consistent and whether the whole thing is interesting and logical." In "Characters" (June 1925), Richardson proposed that "the peasant class of the Negro group" contained that element that was sufficiently "different and interesting" to make good theater. Finally, in "The Unpleasant Play" (September 1925), he spoke directly to black writers and urged them to "make his audience hear the truth, or nothing."

W. E. B. Du Bois echoed Richardson's beliefs in a July 1926 article in the *Crisis,* in which he laid out the four principles for a "Negro Theatre":

Playbill for Willis Richardson's play, *The Chip Woman's Fortune.*

Negro theatre must be:

I.   About Us. That is, they must have plots which reveal Negro life as it is.

II.   By us. That is, they must be written by Negro authors who understand from birth and continual association just what it means to be a Negro today.

III.   For us. That is, the theater must cater primarily to Negro audiences and be supported and sustained by their entertainment and approval.

IV.   Near Us. The theater must be in a Negro neighborhood near the mass of ordinary Negro people.

Out of Du Bois's call came the Krigwa Players and the Harlem Experimental Theater — stock companies that performed plays in the basement of the 135th Street Branch Library. The Krigwa Little Negro Theatre Movement was founded in 1925 by Du Bois and a group of writers, some from the *Crisis*. The group, originally called the Crigwa, or Crisis Guild of Writers and Artists, was assembled from those who sent in manuscripts for the Spingarn Prizes in literature and art. Krigwa branches were also formed in other cities, including Washington, D.C. Although short-lived, the Krigwa Little Negro Theatre Movement helped to stimulate the formation and activity of many other small theater groups. Two years later, the Harlem Experimental Theater was formed. Cofounders included Rose McClendon, Dorothy Peterson, Regina M. Andrews, Benjamin Locke, and Jessie Fauset. Performances were held at St. Philips

**Krigwa Players
productions in Harlem:**

*The Broken Banjo*

*Compromise*

*Foreign Mail*

*Her*

*The Fool's Errand*

*Blue Blood*

**Harlem Experimental
Theater productions
of plays by black
playwrights:**

*Plumes*

*A Sunny Morning*

*Duchess Says Her Prayers*

*The No Count Boy*

*Little Stone Ladder*

*Prodigal Son*

*Rider of Dreams*

*Climbing Jacob's Ladder*

**LIVING THEATER**
Perhaps more than anywhere else the best theater in the black community could be found in Harlem's churches. In these places black men took orthodox Christian theology and Old and New Testament stories and transformed them into original and powerful oratory performances.

**"The [Negro playwright's] audience is more than a double audience. His audience is always both white America and black America. . . . The Negro author can try the experiment of putting black America in the orchestra chairs, so to speak, and keeping white America in the gallery, but he is likely at any moment to find his audience shifting places on him, and sometimes without notice."**

— James Weldon Johnson, "The Dilemma of the Negro Author,"
*American Mercury*, December 1928

Episcopal Church and the 135th Street Branch Library. In 1929 the Negro Art Theatre was born at the Abysinnian Baptist Church, as were the Harlem Community Players at the 135th Street Branch (now known as the Countee Cullen Regional Branch). During these years African-American stock companies produced good plays and developed some excellent actors, a number of whom later performed on Broadway or in the movies. These companies, however, could not compete with the lure and financial power of Broadway and vaudeville, so they found themselves constantly wanting for performers.

*Young Man in a Vest*, William H. Johnson, *c.* 1939-1940.

# AGAINST ALL ODDS

## VISUAL ARTISTS AND THEIR STRUGGLE FOR RECOGNITION

My aim is to express in a natural way
what I feel both rhythmically and spiritually,
all that has been saved up in my family
of primitiveness and tradition.

— Painter WILLIAM H. JOHNSON

## BEATING THE ODDS

BEFORE 1920, if you were black and wanted to create art, America was not the place to do it. Europe, on the other hand, welcomed African-American artists. Galleries and museums displayed their work, and investors purchased it. Two famous black artists before the Harlem Renaissance — Henry Ossawa Tanner and Edmonia Lewis — both made their living across the Atlantic.

In the United States, African Americans were not simply discouraged from the visual arts; they were frozen out. Most art schools refused to accept blacks, while libraries, art galleries, and museums did not display their work and made black visitors feel unwelcome. White organizations that did focus on black issues believed that African Americans needed to devote their energies toward uplifting their economic status, not wasting their time in the trivial pursuit of fine arts.

Meta Warrick Fuller
*Ethiopa Awakening,* 1914.

## "Let us train ourselves to see beauty in 'black.'"

The first to break from the exile tradition and to return to the United States was sculptor Meta Warrick Fuller. She left Europe, where she had been studying with Auguste Rodin. After she made her home in the United States, she created sculptures that resonated in African heritage, ethnic pride, and folk background. By exploring African-American and African culture, Fuller's work became a blueprint for black artists of the next generation. Her two finest works, *Ethiopia Awakening* (1914) and *Mary Turner: A Silent Protest Against Mob Violence* (1919), are among the earliest examples of American art to reflect an influence from African sculpture. The sculptures also challenged the racist political and social climate of the period. Based more on Egyptian traditions than West African, *Ethiopia Awakening* resembles a funerary statue but breaks from the stiff profiles of Egyptian art by portraying the woman's head in movement, as if awakening from the deep sleep of the past to glimpse a new beginning for black people in America. She followed this sculpture with her more politically explicit work, *Mary Turner: A Silent Protest Against Mob Violence*. This sculpture was inspired by the lynching of Mary Turner in Valdosta, Georgia, after she was accused of plotting with her husband and a friend to murder a white man. Fuller's powerful portrayal depicts Mary Turner emerging from a mass of indistinct bodies to symbolize the rising defiance in African Americans.

By the 1920s, Fuller's sculptures had inspired both W. E. B. Du Bois and Alaine Locke to champion African-American and African art. Locke more than Du Bois wrote extensively on the subject. In an essay in *The New Negro* titled "The Legacy of the Ancestral Art, Locke wrote:

[T]he Negro is not a cultural foundling without his inheritance. Our timid and apologetic imitativeness and overburdening sense of cultural indebtedness have, let us hope, their natural end in such knowledge and realization . . . If the forefathers (Africans) could so adroitly master these mediums . . . why not we?

Art was not only a way to express the "New Negro" identity, but it also served as a response to patronizing whites who felt blacks either could not create art or had no business creating it. Locke went even so far as to declare: "[T]he Negro may well become what some have predicted, the artist of American life." Around the same time, James Weldon Johnson asserted that "through artistic efforts the Negro is smashing [an] immemorial stereotype faster than he has ever done . . . impressing upon the national mind the conviction that he is a creator as well as a creature . . . helping to form American civilization."

These influential figures saw art as an important propaganda tool for shaping American consciousness about blacks. W. E. B. Du Bois described his hopes for the creation of new images of African Americans in the following excerpt from a 1920 editorial in *The Crisis*.

Because pervasive racism in America denied blacks a chance to be artists, most creative African Americans found their only venues to be in churches and state fairs, where their work was often displayed with the occupational crafts, such as needlework, made by the handicapped.

It is not that we are ashamed of our color and blood. We are instinctively and almost unconsciously ashamed of the caricatures done of our darker shades. Black as caricature is our half-conscious thought and we shun in print and paint that which we love in life. . . . We remain afraid of black pictures because they are cruel reminders of the crimes of the Sunday 'comics' and 'Nigger' minstrels. Off with these thought chains and inchoate soul-shrinkings, and let us train ourselves to see beauty in 'black.'

Meta Warrick Fuller was the first to realize their desires in her sculptures. During the renaissance, prominent blacks sought to discover and influence the work of other artists who could depict African-American pride.

## FATHER OF BLACK AMERICAN ART

W HILE META WARRICK FULLER set the stage for the artistic renaissance by exploring African and African-American themes, a young artist who moved from Kansas City to Harlem in 1924 became the emblem of the "New Negro" possibility. His name was Aaron Douglas.

Douglas was often called the "official" artist of the Harlem Renaissance, or the "Father of Black American Art." Alain Locke dubbed him a "pioneering Africanist." Though these titles are perhaps exaggerated, Douglas was without question the most celebrated and successful of Harlem's visual artists in the 1920s. He was lured to New York by James Weldon Johnson, editor of the

Edwin Augustus Harleston's portrait of Aaron Douglas, 1899-1979; Douglas's mural *Aspects of Negro Life* was commisioned by the 135th Street Branch of the New York Public Library in 1934.

Urban League's *Opportunity* and one of the era's most tireless boosters. Soon after arriving, Douglas met German artist Winold Reiss, who challenged Douglas to shed his academic style and look at the design and compositional elements of African art. Around the same time, Douglas also met white Philadelphia art collector Albert Barnes. Barnes, who had contributed to Alain Locke's anthology *The New Negro,* was one of the first Americans to collect Modern European artists, such as Picasso, Matisse, and Gaugin, as well as West African sculpture. Through Barnes, Douglas studied African and modern art up close when few in America were even aware of either. From his exposure, Douglas borrowed the modernist's shallow depth of field, the monochromatic palette of Analytic Cubism, and the simple and stylized lines of African sculpture. The work that resulted came to embody all that the Harlem Renaissance stood for — the culturally rich aspects of African-American life and heritage.

Aaron Douglas illustrated many books during the 1920s. Perhaps the most celebrated of Douglas's works were his illustrations for James Weldon Johnson's book of poems, *God's Trombones*, 1926. Right, Douglas drew *Listen, Lord — A Prayer* for the opening poem of the collection.

Douglas's exploration of African aesthetics and his use of black themes brought him to the attention of many of the era's movers and shakers. Du Bois hired him often to illustrate covers and interior pages of the *Crisis*. James Weldon Johnson did the same at *Opportunity*. He also contributed to such national magazines as *Harper's, Vanity Fair,* and *Theater Arts Magazine*. The 135th Street Branch invited him to create a mural in its lobby. And major book publishing companies asked him to illustrate a number of important books, including Carl Van Vechten's notorious *Nigger Heaven*.

## THREE ARTISTS DEFY THE ODDS AND DEFINE THE TIMES

DESPITE AARON DOUGLAS'S seeming corner on the artistic market of the 1920s, a number of other artists also came of age during the period. Three artists of note who emerged from the era to make their names in the decades that followed were sculptor Augusta Savage and painters Palmer C. Hayden and William H. Johnson. They epitomized the struggle African Americans still faced in order to market their art. To make ends meet, Augusta Savage found herself working as a laundress, Palmer C.

### HARMON FOUNDATION

The Harmon Foundation, formed in 1923 to support African-American achievement, held its first art competition in 1926. It was the first and only organization of the era to offer recognition to black visual artists. At the time, the Harmon exhibitions were the largest and most publicized effort to encourage African-American artists and show what they were creating. The foundation often came under criticism for lumping together all types of art by artists of all levels of ability and presenting them as "Negro art" simply because the artists were black. Still, the Harmon Foundation was influential in launching the careers of Palmer C. Hayden, the winner of its first contest, and William H. Johnson, who came in second place. Both used their prize money to travel to Paris to study art.

Hayden stinted as a janitor, and William H. Johnson had a number of menial jobs. In spite of these hardships, they persevered, and nearly every hour that they weren't working they spent sculpting and painting. Because they spent what little free time they had in their studios, these artists essentially missed the renaissance. They did not socialize at Dark Tower soirees, attend Broadway musicals, or dance the night away at the Savoy Ballroom. Their dedication and persistence, however, made it easier for the next generation's black artists, such as Romare Bearden and Jacob Lawrence, to garner public recognition and patronage.

### AUGUSTA SAVAGE, 1892–1962

SAVAGE SPENT HER days working hard in Manhattan steam laundries to support her infirm parents and extended families, and spent her nights absorbed in the advocacy of black people by creating powerful art. She made her name by sculpting a bust of W. E. B. Du Bois in 1923. She went on to create small clay portraits of ordinary African Americans that portrayed their quiet dignity. Her ability to capture the energy of everyday black life extended Meta Warrick Fuller's efforts to illustrate African-American culture with large social and political symbols.

A popular image of the Harlem Renaissance was the African-American youth, because he or she embodied all the hope wrapped up in the "New Negro" philosophy.

*Green Apples*, Augusta Savage, 1930.

### PALMER C. HAYDEN, 1890–1973

HAYDEN CAME TO prominence as the first winner of the Harmon Foundation art competition in 1926. At the time, Hayden was the Foundation's janitor, which raised protests of nepotism and amateurism in the organization. Hayden's winning paint-ing, *Fetíche et Fleurs* (1926), embodied Alain Locke's belief that African art was crucial as the foundation for creating original African-American art. The majority of Hayden's work, however, was typically centered on black-American life, legends, and folk heroes. His canvases often portrayed Harlem street life or recounted customs, love, and small-town folks from his native Virginia and West Virginia, where he worked on the railroad before going to war. He was criticized for lapsing into a portrayal of blacks that seemed rooted in cultural stereotypes. His insistence on portraying blacks with the masks of minstrels was an ever-conscious reminder that no matter how isolated they were from white culture, blacks were performing for a white audience.

*Fetíche et Fleurs*, Palmer Hayden, 1926.

## WILLIAM H. JOHNSON, 1901–1970

JOHNSON BEGAN HIS career as an academic painter, but as his art matured he shed his learned realism for a deliberate primitivism. His conscious creation of a naïve, childlike style painted in bright colors often seemed crude and awkward, as if he had not been trained at all, but in fact his paintings were deeply influenced by the work of Vincent Van Gogh, Edvard Munch, and Chaim Soutine. His work contained the Expressionist quality of broad, emotional paint strokes and bright colors that was very much informed by his exposure to European Modernism. Many African-American critics, however, were put off by Johnson's technique because he seemed to them to be reinforcing cultural stereotypes of the ignorant, unskilled Negro rather than the cultured "New Negro" they were so committed to promoting.

Shortly after winning the 1930 Harmon gold medal for his painting *Jacobia Hotel,* which depicted a building in his hometown of Florence, North Carolina, Johnson was arrested by the local police. No one knows whether it was owing to the embarrassing fact that the Jacobia Hotel was a brothel or to the backlash at Johnson's achieving national recognition.

Above, *Self Portrait*, William H. Johnson, 1930; left, *Jacobia Hotel*, 1930.

123

## THE PHOTOGRAPHER OF
## THE HARLEM RENAISSANCE

JAMES VANDERZEE'S PHOTOGRAPHS epitomized everything that the "New Negro" stood for. His work in a sense legitimized black urban immigrants' pride in their identity. African Americans from all walks of life entered VanDerZee's studio to record the important events of their lives. For his part, VanDerZee made sure that each photograph captured the extraordinary sense of self-esteem, style, and optimism that emanated from Harlemites in the 1920s.

VanDerZee, 1886-1983, would go to great lengths to create a portrait that embodied an orderly, prosperous bourgeois life, far removed from the indignities and injustices of the past. To this end, VanDerZee attended to every detail. He followed certain social rules in each photograph: Women's legs were crossed, their backs straight. Then, he would add touches to convey an almost defiant confidence: the collar of a coat turned up or a hat pulled stylishly over one eye. Most important, his subjects had to be flawless even if in real life that were not the case. To ensure this, VanDerZee would touch up the photographs so that a frayed collar or missing button did not show. He would smooth out skin color, straighten teeth, or even sketch in a few extra pieces of jewelry.

When not in his studio, VanDerZee roamed the streets of Harlem and bore witness to the entire renaissance. In his photographs he captured Harlem's weddings, funerals, and parades, as well as bridge clubs, fraternities, school groups, and church functions. He photographed Harlem's sights: famed patron A'Lelia Walker's Dark Tower, a chic salon of artists and socialites; the Reverend Adam Clayton Powell Sr.'s Abyssinian Baptist Church; the elaborate, complex ceremonies of Marcus Garvey's UNIA; or the Theresa Hotel, which in the days of segre-

**His subjects had to be flawless even if in real life that were not the case.**

gated residences was one of the country's finest black hostelries. VanDerZee ensured Harlem's denizens and locations were memorialized for posterity.

Though the visuals arts could be considered a stepchild of the renaissance, clearly the advances in recognition and respect that visual artists achieved was unprecedented in the white, elistist world of modern art at the time. Through their art, these artists put America on notice that black themes — the lives, activities, and portraits of African Americans — were a legitimate, valuable, and unique part of American life, and that black artists deserved recognition and patronage equal to any other artist.

A 1930s demonstration in Harlem.

# RAGE IN THE STREETS

## THE WANING OF THE RENAISSANCE
## AND THE BEGINNING OF THE HARLEM RIOTS

I've lived a life
but nothin' I've gained.
Each day I'm full
of sorrow and pain.

No one seems to care
enough for me
to give me a word
of sympathy.

Oh, me! Oh, my!
Wonder what will
the end be?
Oh, me! Oh, my!
Wonder what will
become of poor me?

— "Wasted Life Blues,"
words and music by BESSIE SMITH

127

## BLACK TUESDAY

T
UESDAY, OCTOBER 29, 1929, marked the end of the Roaring Twenties and the
beginning of the Great Depression. This was the day the stock market crashed. In
the weeks afterward, it seemed as if only investors in the market would be affected.
Uptown, Harlemites looked upon the crash from a bemused distance. Since most African
Americans had not invested in stocks and bonds, they viewed the crash as a white problem. When newspapers began calling October 29 "Black Tuesday," African Americans
only saw irony. Now whites would learn what it was like to be black in America — poor.

Uptown, with Prohibition still in full swing, the speakeasies and nightclubs of Harlem
continued to draw crowds. On Broadway, musicals such as Fats Waller's *Hot Chocolates*
and plays like Wallace Thurman's blockbuster *Harlem* opened to packed houses. On the
literary front, 1927 and 1928 were boom years, and the future appeared just as promising.
But by the end of 1930 that optimism had expired. The nail in the coffin, however, did not
come until two years later, when Prohibition was repealed and whites no longer had to
travel uptown to drink alcohol. Stride pianist Willie "the Lion" Smith said it was legal
liquor that did to Harlem what scarcer tips and shuttered warehouses had failed to do.

In the 1930s, 24 international unions barred blacks from membership. Below, a line for unemplyment registration.

> "It was legal liquor that did to Harlem what scarcer tips
> and shuttered warehouses had failed to do."
>
> — Stride pianist Willie "the Lion" Smith

## "LAST HIRED, FIRST FIRED!"

THE FIRST TO feel the effects of the Great Depression were the laborers and kitchen mechanics who worked low-wage jobs and paid high rents to live in Harlem. The phrase "Last Hired, First Fired" came to mean that black workers would lose their jobs long before whites would join in the unemployment lines. Many of these people could not find new jobs. A February 1930 edition of the New York *Herald Tribune* reported that the stock market crash had "produced five times as much unemployment in Harlem as in other parts of the city." By 1932 the median family income in Harlem had plummeted 43.6 percent, from $1,808 to $1,019 ($13,379 in today's dollars), while unemployment reached nearly 50 percent. As well, a new kind of slave market arose at the corner of 167th Street and Jerome Avenue in the Bronx, where African-American women waited to be "rented" at day rates for housework. These women worked for ten to twenty cents an hour, considerably less than the fifty cents an hour they'd been earning prior to the Depression. Under these dire economic conditions, Harlem changed from an oasis of black pride into a slum, where two and three families lived in a single apartment and buildings became run-down from the stress of so many tenants.

### HOT BEDS

The term "hot bed" came into use to describe a bed that was rented out in shifts. A night worker slept in the bed during the day, while a day laborer rested in it at night — the same room, the same bed, the same sheets, the same bedbugs.

## MINORITY EMPLOYMENT FROM 1930–1935

| COMPANY | WHITE EMPLOYEES | BLACK EMPLOYEES |
| --- | --- | --- |
| Consolidated Gas Company | 10,000 | 213 porters |
| New York Edison Company | 10,000 | 65 porters, cleaners, and hall men |
| New York Telephone Company | 10,000 | 65 laborers |
| IRT Subway Company | 10,000 | 580 messengers, porters, and cleaners |

129

## HARLEM CHURCHES HELP

W HEN THE GOVERNMENT failed to meet the needs of all the hungry, the homeless, and the jobless, many African-American churches stepped in to help. Adam Clayton Powell Sr. preached from the pulpit of his Abyssinian Baptist Church, "We clothe God by Clothing men and women. . . . When you give men and women coats, shoes, and dresses, you are giving clothes to God." He went on to "give one thousand dollars of [his] salary during the next three months to help relieve this terrible unemployment situation." In the first three months of 1931, the Abyssinian Baptist Relief Bureau served 28,500 free meals and distributed 525 food baskets, 17,928 pieces of clothing, and 2,564 pairs of shoes. Other churches helped out as well, running employment agencies, shelters, and soup kitchens for the needy.

Line of children receiving food from nuns.

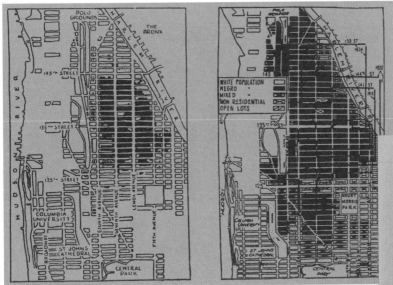

**1925**

**1930**

By 1930, Harlem had grown more than 600 percent since 1900 to more than 350,000 people, with an average density of 233 persons per acre, compared with 133 per acre for the rest of Manhattan.

## EXODUS

"WE WERE NO longer in vogue, anyway, we Negroes," commented Langston Hughes before he left Harlem for his mother's home in Cleveland in 1931. One year later, Hughes would leave the country to make a film with other black artists in the former U.S.S.R. Though this film was never actually shot, the fact that Hughes and others felt more hope in an uncertain project halfway across the world suggests just how grim America had become for African Americans.

By 1935, almost no one from the renaissance's glory days was left in Harlem. The economic fallout from the Depression was the biggest reason for this breakup, but it was not the sole cause. Throughout the renaissance cracks had existed under the surface. These divisions, however, were easily overlooked when the money and recognition were plentiful. Once opportunity disappeared, the artists of the renaissance began to divide more clearly into two camps. The younger artists believed the arts should celebrate blackness in all its variety and be truthful to life, whereas the older, more established ones felt the arts should function as propaganda to uplift the status of African Americans. A defining moment came with the success of Wallace Thurman's play *Harlem*. To supporters of black theater groups such as the Krigwa Players, Thurman's play was like a slap in the face. *Harlem* celebrated a part of black life — the rent party, with its bootleg liquor, gambling, and erotic dancing — that many of the Talented Tenth would rather have gone unknown to the larger white population. Though these divisions had nothing to do with the Depression, they made it impossible for African Americans to face the economic disaster with a unified front. Consequently, the Harlem Renaissance disintegrated and its participants scattered.

- Arna Bontemps moved to Nashville to join the faculty of Fisk University.
- Countee Cullen returned in 1934 to De Witt Clinton High School in Manhattan, from which he had graduated, to teach French for the rest of his life. Among his students was future writer James Baldwin, who interviewed Cullen for the school newspaper.
- Aaron Douglas joined Charles Spurgeon Johnson on the faculty at Fisk University in Nashville, Tennessee, and remained there until his death.
- W. E. B. Du Bois stopped publishing literary works and struggled to keep the *Crisis* afloat by refusing his salary.
- Jessie Fauset left her editorship at the *Crisis,* married an insurance broker, and became a housewife in Brooklyn.
- Zora Neale Hurston returned to the South, where she collected folktales for *Mules and Men* (1935) and wrote one of her finest novels, *Their Eyes Were Watching God* (1937).
- James Weldon Johnson joined the faculty at Fisk University in Nashville.
- Alain Locke increasingly turned his gaze toward Howard University in Washington, D.C., where he was a faculty member.
- Claude McKay lived in poverty and worked for the WPA during the Depression.
- Wallace Thurman, battling tuberculosis and alcoholism, died in poverty in 1934.
- Jean Toomer became a follower of the religious mystic Gurdjieff.

## NEGROES

Oh, Lawd, I dones forgot Harlem!

Say, you colored folks, hungry a long time in 135th Street —
they got swell music at the Waldorf-Astoria. It sure is a mighty nice place to
shake hips in, too. There's dancing after supper in a big warm room. It's cold as
hell on Lenox Avenue. All you've had all day is a cup of coffee. Your pawnshop
overcoat's a ragged banner on your hungry frame. You know, downtown folks
are just crazy about Paul Robeson! maybe they'll like you, too, black mob from
Harlem. Drop in at the Waldorf this afternoon for tea. Stay for dinner. Give Park
Avenue a log of darkie color — free for nothing! Ask the junior Leaguers to sing
a spiritual for you. They probably know 'em better than you do — and their
lips won't be so chapped with cold after they step out of their closed cars in
undercover driveways.

*Hallelujah! Undercover driveways!*

*Ma soul's a witness for de Waldorf-Astoria!*

(A thousand nigger section-hands keep the roadbeds smooth,

so investments in railroads pay ladies with diamond

necklaces staring at Cert murals.)

*Thank God A-mighty!*

(And a million niggers bend their backs on rubber plantations,

for rich behinds to ride on thick tires to the

Theatre Guild tonight.)

*Ma soul's a witness!*

(And here we stand, shivering in the cold, in Harlem.)

*Glory be to God–*

*De Waldorf-Astoria's open!*

— LANGSTON HUGHES, New Masses, December 1931

## HARLEM RIOT, 1935

WITH MANY OF the Talented Tenth gone, Harlem became a slum populated predominantly by the unskilled and undereducated, who were unemployed or underemployed. At the same time, blacks from the South continued to come North because the conditions on the farms were even worse. In this increasingly over-crowded community the streets of Harlem became a powder keg ready to explode. The igniting spark would come in March of 1935. With more than fifty percent of the African Americans in Harlem receiving unemployment relief, frustration and bitterness had reached an all-time high. Along 125th Street, the stores that had catered to blacks refused to hire them. When a youth attempted to steal a ten-cent pocketknife and was arrested, the response was incendiary.

*THE NEW YORK TIMES*, MARCH 21, 1935

### TROOPS GUARD HARLEM: MAYOR PLEADS FOR PEACE

Crowds of restless Negro residents and thousands of curious white visitors thronged Harlem's sidewalks last night under the sharp watch of more than 500 policemen, but there were no new outbreaks such as kept the district in turmoil all Tuesday night and early yesterday morning. Of the 100 or more white men and Negroes who were shot, stabbed, clubbed or stoned during the rioting of Tuesday night, only a handful remained in Harlem hospitals. These however were on the critical list. Up to last night there was only one death as a result of the rioting. While the police seemed certain that they had enough men in the district to put down any new uprising of the hoodlum element that looted stores and broke more than 300 shopwindows during the rioting, the Merchants Association of Harlem telegraphed to Governor Lehman that the police force was inadequate and made a plea for "military assistance."

## LEGACY

THE IMPORTANCE OF the Harlem Renaissance cannot be underestimated. By the end of the 1930s, jazz had clearly become America's music, while the jitterbug, a Savoy Ballroom invention, had taken the country by storm and changed couples dancing. Young African-American writers who had learned their craft from renaissance authors began to make a name for themselves. Richard Wright, Alice Walker, Ralph Ellison, Gwendolyn Brooks, and James Baldwin would all come out of Harlem in the coming decades to write some of America's greatest books — Wright's *Native Son*, Walker's *The Color Purple*, Ellison's *Invisible Man*, Brooks's *Annie Allen*, and Baldwin's *Go Tell It on the Mountain*. "Black is Beautiful," a phrase with roots in the Harlem Renaissance, would become a rallying cry in the civil rights movement decades later. In the end, the seeds sown during the Harlem Renaissance are still bearing fruit, not just for African Americans, but for all Americans.

I've known rivers:
I've known rivers ancient as the world
and older than the flow of human blood
in human veins.
    My soul has grown deep like the rivers.
I bathed in the Euphrates when dawns
            were young.
I built my hut beside the Congo and
        it lulled me to sleep.
I looked upon the Nile and raised the
        pyramids above it.
I heard the singing of the Mississippi
        when Abe Lincoln went down
        to New Orleans,
and I've seen its muddy bosom
        turn all golden in the sunset.
I've known rivers:
ancient, dusky rivers.
My soul has grown deep
        like the rivers.
                From memory to read
            on radio show —
                Langston Hughes

# BIBLIOGRAPHY

Adoff, Arnold, ed. *The Poetry of Black America: Anthology of the 20th Century.* New York: Harper & Row, 1973.

*African American Almanac.* Detroit: Gale Research, 1994.

*Against the Odds: The Artists of the Harlem Renaissance.* Alexandria, Va.: PBS Video, 1993. Videocassette.

Anderson, Jervis. *This Was Harlem: A Cultural Portrait 1900–1950.* New York: Farrar, Straus & Giroux, 1982.

Andrews, William L., ed. *Classic Fiction of the Harlem Renaissance.* New York: Oxford University Press, 1994.

Asante, Melefi K. *The Historical and Cultural Atlas of African Americans.* New York: Macmillan, 1991.

Bardolph, Richard. *The Negro Vanguard.* New York: Vintage, 1961.

Bearden, Romare, and Harry Henderson. *A History of African-American Artists: From 1792 to the Present.* New York: Pantheon, 1993.

Bergman, Peter M. *The Chronological History of the Negro in America.* New York: Harper & Row, 1969.

Bontemps, Arna. *The Harlem Renaissance Remembered.* New York: Dodd, Mead, 1972.

Candaele, Kerry. *Milestones in Black American History: Bound for Glory, 1910–1930*. New York: Chelsea House, 1997.

Christian, Charles M. *Black Saga: The African American Experience: A Chronology*. Washington, D.C.: Civitas Counterpoint, 1999.

Ciment, James. *Atlas of African American History*. New York: Checkmark Books, 2001.

*Civil Rights Since 1787: A Reader on the Black Struggle*. New York: New York University Press, 2000.

Cullen, Countee. *My Soul's High Song: The Collected Writings of Countee Cullen*. Edited by Gerald Early. New York: Anchor Books, 1991.

Curtain, Patricia R. *I Too Am American, Documents from 1619 to Present*. New York: Publishers Co., 1970.

*Definitive Dixieland Collection: 73 Songs*. Milwaukee, Wis.: Hal Leonard Publishing Co., 1993.

Douglas, Ann. *Terrible Honesty: Mongrel Manhattan in the 1920s*. New York: Noonday, 1995.

Earle, Jonathan. *The Routledge Atlas of African American History*. New York: Routledge, 2000.

Favor, J. Martin. *Authentic Blackness: The Folk in the New Negro Renaissance*. Durham, N.C.: Duke University Press, 1999.

*Fire!! Devoted to Younger Negro Artists*. Westport, Conn.: Negro University Press, 1970.

Fishel, Leslie H. *The Black Americans: A Documentary History*. Glenview, Ill.: Scott Foresman, 1970.

Foner, Philip S., ed. *The Voice of Black America: Major Speeches by Negroes in the United States, 1797–1971*. New York: Simon & Schuster, 1972.

*From These Roots: A Review of the "Harlem Renaissance."* New York: William Greaves Productions, 1974.

Gossett, Thomas F. *Race: The History of an Idea in America*. New York: Oxford University Press, 1997.

Groce, Nancy. *New York: Songs of the City*. New York: Watson-Guptill, 1999.

Harris, M. A. *A Negro History Tour of Manhattan*. New York: Greenwood, 1968.

Harris, Middleton. *The Black Book*. New York: Random House, 1974.

Harris, Trudier, ed. *Dictionary of Literary Biography: Afro-American Writers from the Harlem Renaissance to 1940*. Detroit, Mich.: Gale Research, 1987.

Haskins, Jim. *The Cotton Club*. New York: New American Library, 1984.

Hasse, John E., ed. *Jazz: The First Century*. New York: William Morrow, 2000.

Hill, Anthony D. *Pages from the Harlem Renaissance: A Chronicle of Performance*. New York: Peter Lang Publishers, 1996.

Holland, Marie Juanita, ed. *Narratives of African American Art and Identity: The David C. Driskell Collection*. Rohnert Park, Calif.: Pomegranate, 1998.

Hollinger, David A. *Postethnic America*. New York: Basic Books, 1995.

Huggins, Nathan Irvin. *Harlem Renaissance*. New York: Oxford University Press, 1971.

———, ed. *Voices from the Harlem Renaissance*. New York: Oxford University Press, 1995.

Hughes, Langston. *Book of Rhythms*. New York: Oxford UP, 1995.

———. *The Collected Poems of Langston Hughes*. New York: Knopf, 1994.

———. *Famous Negro Music Makers*. New York: Dodd, Mead, 1955.

———. *The First Book of Jazz*. New York: F. Watts, 1955.

———, and Milton Meltzer. *Black Magic: A Pictorial History of the African-American in the Performing Arts*. New York: De Capo Press, 1990.

———. *A Pictorial History of the Negro in America,* 3rd rev. ed. New York: Crown, 1969.

*I'll Make My World*. Vols. 1–6. Alexandria, Va.: PBS Video, 1999. Videocassette.

Johnson, Eloise E. *Rediscovering the Harlem Renaissance: The Politics of Exclusion*. New York: Garland, 1997.

Johnson, James Weldon. *The Autobiography of an Ex-Coloured Man*. New York: Knopf, 1927.

———. *Black Manhattan*. New York: Knopf, 1930.

————. *God's Trombones: Seven Negro Sermons in Verse*. New York: Viking, 1927.

————, ed. *The Book of American Negro Poetry*. New York: Harcourt, Brace, 1922.

Katz, William Loren. *Eyewitness: A Living Documentary of the African American Contribution to American History*. New York: Simon & Schuster, 1995.

Kellner, Bruce, ed. *The Harlem Renaissance: A Historical Dictionary for the Era*. Westport, Conn.: Greenwood Press, 1984.

Kirschke, Amy Helene. *Aaron Douglas: Art, Race, and the Harlem Renaissance*. Jackson: University Press of Mississippi, 1995.

Kramer, Victor, ed. *The Harlem Renaissance Re-examined*. New York: AMS Press, 1987.

Lewis, David Levering. *W. E. B. Du Bois: Biography of a Race 1868–1919*. New York: Henry Holt, 1993.

————. *When Harlem Was in Vogue*. New York: Oxford University Press, 1981.

————, ed. *The Portable Harlem Renaissance Reader*. New York: Viking, 1994.

Locke, Alain, ed. *The New Negro: Voices of the Harlem Renaissance*. New York: Touchstone, 1997.

Magill, Frank N., ed. *Masterpiece of African-American Literature*. New York: HarperCollins, 1992.

Miers, Charles. *Harlem Renaissance: Art of Black America*. New York: Abrams, 1994.

Mitchell, Loften. *Black Drama: The Story of the American Negro in the Theatre*. New York: Hawthorne Books, 1967.

*New York Public Library African American Desk Reference*. New York: Wiley, 1999.

Osofsky, Gilbert. *Harlem: The Making of a Ghetto*. 2nd ed. New York: Harper Torchbooks, 1970.

Ottley, Roi, and William Weatherby. *The Negro in New York*. New York: New York Public Library, 1967.

Ovington, Mary White. *Black and White Sat Down Together*. New York: Feminist Press, 1995.

Patterson, Lindsay. *The Negro Music and Art*. New York: Publishers Co., 1969.

Perry, Margaret. *Harlem Renaissance: Annotated Bibliography and Commentary.* New York: Garland, 1982.

Quarles, Benjamin. *The Negro in the Making of America.* New York: Collier Books, 1964.

Randall, Dudley. *The Black Poets.* New York: Bantam Books, 1970.

*Rhapsodies in Black: Art of the Harlem Renaissance.* Berkeley: University of California Press, 1999.

Resh, Richard. *Black America: Accommodation and Confrontation in the Twentieth Century.* Lexington, Mass.: D. C. Heath, 1989.

Reynolds, Gary A., and Beryl J. Wright. *Against the Odds: African-American Artists and the Harmon Foundation.* Newark, N.J.: Newark Museum, 1989.

Ross, Leon T., and Kenneth A. Mimms. *African American Almanac: Day-by-Day Black History.* Jefferson, N.C.: McFarland, 1997.

Sampson, Henry T. *The Ghost Walks: A Chronological History of Blacks in Show Business 1865–1910.* Metuchen, N.J.: Scarecrow Press, 1988.

Sanders, Leslie Catherine. *The Development of Black Theater in America.* Baton Rouge: Louisiana State University Press, 1988.

Scheiner, Seth M. *Negro Mecca: A History of the Negro in New York City 1865–1920.* New York: New York University Press, 1965.

Schoener, Allon. *Harlem on My Mind: Cultural Capital of Black America 1900–1968.* New York: Random House, 1968.

VanDerZee, James. *The World of James VanDerZee: A Visual Record of Black Americans.* New York: Grove, 1969.

Ward, Geoffrey C., and Ken Burns. *Jazz: A History of America's Music.* New York: Knopf, 2000.

Watson, Steven. *Harlem Renaissance: Hub of African American Culture, 1920–1930.* New York: Pantheon, 1995.

*W. E. B. Du Bois: A Biography in Four Voices.* San Francisco: California Newsreel, 1995. Videocassette.

*W. E. B. Du Bois of Great Barrington.* Alexandria, Va.: PBS Video, 1999. Videocassette.

Wedin, Carolyn. *Inheritors of the Spirit: Mary White Ovington and the Founding of the NAACP*. New York: Wiley, 1998.

Wesley, Charles H. *The Quest for Equality, from Civil War to Civil Rights*. New York: Publishers Co., 1970.

Willis, Deborah. *Reflections in Black: A History of Black Photographers, 1840 to the Present*. New York: W. W. Norton, 2000.

Wilson, Sandra K., ed. *The Crisis Reader: Stories, Poetry, and Essays from the NAACP's Crisis Magazine*. New York: Modern Library, 1999.

Wintz, Cary D. *Black Culture and the Harlem Renaissance*. Houston, Tex.: Rice University Press, 1988.

———, ed., *The Harlem Renaissance 1920–1940*. Vols. 1-7. New York: Garland, 1996.

*The WPA Guide to New York City: The Federal Writers' Project Guide to 1930s New York*. New York: Pantheon, 1982.

# INDEX

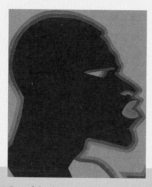

# CREDITS

Grateful acknowledgement is made to the following for permission to reprint previously published material.

Harold Ober Associates Incorporated: First published in New Masses.
Copyright © 1931 by Langston Hughes: "Negroes."
Greenwood Publishing Group Inc., Westport, CT: "Harlem Jive."
Children's Press/Franklin Watts, a division of Scholastic Inc.: "Ten Basic Elements of Jazz" from *The First Book of Jazz* by Langston Hughes.

ILLUSTRATION CREDITS

Pages ii, 111, 135, Courtesy of Culver Pictures

Pages vi, 93 bottom, 94, 95, 97 left and right, 98-99, Courtesy of Frank Driggs

Pages vii top and center, 4, 7, 13, 17, 21 top and bottom, 26, 44, 47 48 top and bottom, 50, 51, 58 top, 64, 65, 66 right, 67, 71 left and right, 72 left and right, 73 left and right, 86, 89, 102, 105, 106, 107, 108, 120, 121 right, 143, 146, 147, Courtesy of Yale Collection of American Literature, Beinecke Rare Book and Manuscript Library

Pages vii bottom, 114, 123 left and right, Courtesy of Smithsonian American Art Museum

Page viii, Courtesy of Emmet Collection, Miriam and Ira D. Wallach Division of Art, Prints and Photographs, The New York Public Library, Astor, Lenox and Tildon Foundations

Pages ix, 6 bottom left, 9, 18, 32, 35 right, 39 right and left, 43, 58 bottom, 81, 83, 126, 128, 132, Courtesy of Photograph and Prints Division, Schomburg Center for Research in Black Culture, The New York Public Library, Astor, Lenox and Tilden Foundations

Pages 6 top right, 8, 10, 16, 22, 25, 27, 56 (Photo by Gordon Parks), 96 and 101 (Illustrations by Miguel Covarrubias), Courtesy of Library of Congress

Page 12, Courtesy of Walter P. Reuther Library, Wayne State University

Page 14, Courtesy of Gwendolyn Knight Lawrence, Courtesy of the Jacob and Gwendolyn Lawrence Foundation

Pages 23 top, 82 top, 84, 85, 124 top and bottom, 125, 130, Photos by James VanDerZee, Courtesy of Donna Mussenden VanDerZee

# BIOGRAPHIES

Laban Carrick Hill has been researching the Harlem Renaissance for more than a decade. *Harlem Stomp!* is the result of this work. The author of nearly twenty novels for young adults, he has also taught writing at Columbia University, Baruch College, and St. Michael's College in Vermont. His poems have been included in the *Contemporary Poetry of New England* anthology and in numerous literary magazines, including the *Tar River Review,* the *Denver Quarterly,* and *American Letters and Commentary.*

Award-winning poet and activist Nikki Giovanni is one of the most beloved and influential writers of our time. In a career spanning more than thirty years, she has produced many books of poetry for children and adults, including *Quilting the Black-Eyed Pea: Poems and Not Quite Poems,* and *Ego-Tripping and Other Poems for Young People.* She is currently a Distinguished Professor of English at Virginia Tech University.

Celebrated illustrator Christopher Myers is the recipient of the Caldecott Honor and the Coretta Scott King Honor Awards for illustration. He has written and illustrated several books for children, including *Harlem: A Poem, Black Cat,* and *Wings.*

# HARLEM STOMP!